The Parish of Largs

by

REV. DAVID B. BAXTER, B.D.

Edited by
MARY B. HALL

© Largs & District Historical Society
All Rights Reserved

ISBN 0 9502751 1 5

THE PARISH OF LARGS

BY
REV. DAVID B BAXTER B. D.

Edited by Mary B Hall

LARGS & DISTRICT HISTORICAL SOCIETY 1992

First published in Great Britain in 1992 by Largs and District Historical Society, Manse Court, Largs, KA30 8AW

No part of this book may be reproduced or transmitted in any form or by any means without the permission in writing from the publisher, except by a reviewer who wishes to quote brief passages in connection with a review for insertion in a magazine, newspaper or broadcast.

British Library Cataloguing-in-Publication Data:
A catalogue record for this book is available from the British Library.

Printed by
Largs Printing Company
120 Main Street, Largs, Ayrshire

The Rev. David B. Baxter, M.A., B.D., Parish Minister of Largs 1928-1929 and Minister of St. Columba's Church of Scotland, Largs, 1929-1965.

Contents

Introduction by Fred Baxter - - - -	vi
Editor's Preface - - - - -	ix
Incumbents - - - - - -	xi
The Parish of Largs - - - - -	1
Notes - - - - - - -	152
Precentors and Organists - - -	157
Appendix - - - - - -	161

Illustrations

Effigy of William de Kilkenni- - - -	5
Skelmorlie Aisle - - - - - -	26
The Old Manse - - - - -	79
Largs Parish Church - - - -	104
Minister and Elders, 1889 - - -	140
Re-dedication of Prophet's Grave - -	165

INTRODUCTION

by Fred Baxter

The Rev. David B. Baxter was minister of St Columba's Church, Largs, from 28th October 1928 to 31st October 1965. He was also – my father.

To a young boy growing up in the Manse with all the privileges and the problems this incurred, early recollections of my father, in retrospect, reflect a lack of the familiarity that one would normally expect.

He was very much a 'stranger' in the house. The man in the big upstairs study, who was always writing copious notes, who answered the telephone, and who made rare appearances at mealtimes to join the family, heading the table in formal fashion, complete with serviette and ring, saying grace; and whose very presence was enough to ensure that three children 'were to be seen but not heard'. He was, incorrectly, held to some extent in awe, and often avoided, – except on a Saturday morning when enough courage would be mustered to approach and ask for a "Saturday Penny", the results varying depending on where and how you got him.

Through childhood and youth the divide of formality lingered, with temporary insights of a closer understanding developing when holiday time arrived. On such occasions over the years a better understanding of the Man, as apart from the Minister emerged.

Of his accomplishments, academic and professional, and his many experiences in life, he never spoke at home. Indeed it was only late in his life, a time when he would frequently reminisce, that I became more aware of his earlier days. I had known he had been a prisoner of war in 1918 when serving with the Royal Scots, but never knew that as a twenty year old, he had been forced to work as a collier down at the coal face in the Rhur, or later, when he became chaplain to the prisoners of war at Munster, he had, at that early age, to preach his first sermon, and to take many funeral services. I also learned that when completing his University career, he had turned down a number of offers, which, had he accepted, would no doubt have led him further afield than the town of Largs.

A zealous worker, a conscientious visitor to all church members throughout the parish, and most capable minister, his service to his church was of a high standard. He became noted as an eloquent preacher and St Columba's Church was often referred to as "Baxter's Kirk".

Like everyone else he had to have his "escapes" and they were to be found either on the billiard table, the bowling green, or the cricket field. His other "escape" was not known to me at the time, and I believe grew during the period of the war when other interests were naturally constrained. That was prolonged research into the lost history of the church in Largs.

Everything of importance in this work was meticulously recorded in great detail, not only in written form, but so far as possible, stored away in his memory. He had an amazing gift – the ability to remember, facts, names, dates etc..

He could remember almost all his congregation, their families, where they lived, who they married and their children. He was familiar with all the many established residences in Largs, all the farm buildings and small holdings in the parish, and was able to recount their predecessors and the history of many.

It was much later in life, I came to realise the implications of all the mountain of notes, scattered around the big study in the manse at Largs. Years of his spare time, historical research in various locations, frequent correspondence with Largs connections in this country and abroad.

Time however, and deterioration in health, ran out on him before he could bring, in some form of completion, the task with which he had been so long involved. It was therefore, thanks to the interest shown by the Largs Historical Society, that all his efforts have not been in vain, and in this centenary year of St Columba's Church Largs a timely publication of his history has been produced. For this achievement I am firstly indebted to the late Mrs Jean Mensing, former Secretary of the Society, who with her keen interest in Largs history, eagerly made the initial moves to bring my father's records to fruition.

It is mainly due to Miss Mary Hall who over recent years,

dedicated long hours of her time to the task of putting "all the pieces of paper" together that this book has been produced.

Those in any way connected with St Columba's church will no doubt find this book of considerable interest; while others may also enjoy a general insight into the Largs of the past, its people, their attitudes and their customs.

EDITOR'S PREFACE

This work is based on the manuscripts donated to Largs & District Historical Society by the family of the late Rev. David Baxter.

Early in the 1940s Mr Baxter wrote:

"I have been at work for some years on the production of a history of Largs. It has been a time-consuming task in the absence of virtually all the original source documents. Unfortunately, the congregational records of the Parish Church do not go back before 1814 and for the earlier period nothing has survived except a few unrelated papers in the 18th century. As a result, the day to day life of the Church is lost forever. In the same way, the records of the old Burgh of Largs are no longer extant, and few relevant documents have so far appeared from collections in private hands. All that can be done is to collect odd scraps of information from varied and often obscure old writings – legal, social and ecclesiastical – and to piece them together in the context of the general historical background. This cannot produce an adequate history of the local past but it does give a sketchy indication of people, events and attitudes which may perhaps be expanded at a later date. Even so, it is only part of my gleanings that I propose to pass on in these lectures, in the hope that time and strength may be granted me to fill them out more acceptably in the better days of peace. The Parish of Largs was for 369 years served by a succession of 25 ministers with an average tenure of almost 15 years. It is appropriate that their story should now be attempted by the 25th on the list since he happens also to close that list for all time. In due course my successor will not be Parish Minister of Largs, but will inaugurate a new series of Ministers of St Columba's Church of Scotland in Largs. And so I turn now to our local annals, grouping them for convenience around the names of the successive ministers in this charge."

Mr Baxter did not complete his History. The commitments of an active parish ministry left little enough time; and even after he retired in October 1965, the task of sorting out the mass of material he had collected became increasingly difficult. He died on 22nd February 1983.

Only a selection from Mr Baxter's papers could be included here, and some explanation for the degree of editing is necessary. Parts of the manuscript existed, generally in the form of lectures which had to be adapted from the spoken to the written word; parts had to be constructed from rough notes. Much of the research was done over 50 years ago, since when new facts have come to light and the approach to local history has altered fundamentally. Within these limits the main narrative follows Mr Baxter's plan, based on the successive ministries and carried up only to 1929 when the Parish of Largs ceased to exist as a separate entity. However, two events from Mr Baxter's later ministry – the 50th anniversary of the present Church and the restoration of "The Prophet's Grave" – have some bearing on the past and are included in an appendix, and in view of Mr Baxter's interest in music, his notes on the precentors and organists who served the Church from 1812 to 1929 have been added.

In preparing the manuscript, I was indebted to many people, especially the late Mrs Jean Mensing, Honorary Secretary of the Largs Historical Society.

Ultimately, of course, the real acknowledgement must be to David Baxter. I am conscious that the work as it now appears is not as he would have presented it. I can only hope that I have succeeded in retrieving something of his dedicated lifelong study of local history.

Mary B Hall.

March 1992

INCUMBENTS OF THE PARISH OF LARGS

WILLIAM DE KILKENNI	1253	– 1256
WILLIAM DE LYNDESAY		1318 Resigned
DAVID NEIL	c. 1563	– 1570
ALEXANDER CALLE	1574	– 1584
WILLIAM FULLERTON	c. 1585	– 1586
WILLIAM COCK	c. 1586	– 1625
THOMAS CRAIG	c. 1631	– 1640
WILLIAM SMITH MA	1644	– 1647
JAMES GLENDINNING MA	1649	– 1658
JOHN WALLACE MA	1658	– 1662
	1672	– 1679
	1687	–
PETER TRUMBLE	fl. 1665	
ALEXANDER GORDON	fl. 1672	
CHARLES LITTLEJOHN MA	1680	– 1688
JOHN WILSON	1689	– 1699
ANDREW CUMIN	1701	– 1742
JOHN CUMIN	1742	– 1743
PATRICK WALLACE MA	1748	– 1755
GILBERT LANG MA	1756	– 1791
STEPHEN ROWAND MA	1792	– 1801
JOHN MITCHELL MD	1802	– 1826
JACOB RICHARDSON	1826	– 1830
JOHN DOW	1831	– 1843
JOHN KINROSS MA	1843	– 1883
JOHN KEITH DD	1885	– 1902
GAVIN LANG PAGAN BD	1902	– 1909
ROBERT OSWALD BD	1910	– 1928
DAVID B BAXTER BD	1928	– 1929

THE PARISH OF LARGS.

The origin of the Parish Church of Largs is lost in obscurity. Yet from the earliest existing records it is associated with the name of St Columba. He came from Ireland in the year 563 to settle on the island of Iona and, from the monastery he founded there on the traditional Irish model, he and his followers journeyed to the mainland and to the adjacent islands as missionaries. The conversions they made and the churches they founded are recorded in placenames all over Scotland. Their number and the wide distances separating them testify to the impress of Columba's remarkable personality and his strenuous life of unremitting Christian activity.

Today, churches dedicated by Columba and churches dedicated by his successors to Columba span the world. He is remembered as the statesman, scholar and man of God who brought the Gospel to much of Scotland and he may well be regarded as the first in the long line of benefactors to whom the parishioners of Largs are indebted for the heritage of Christian worship and the accumulated wealth of Christian living into which they are now entered.

The original church of Largs stood in the old graveyard in the centre of the present town.[1] It was a severely plain building: a rectangular block surmounted by only a modest belfry and, until 1636, minus the more ornate Skelmorlie Aisle which alone survives of the ancient fabric. Unfortunately no exact date can be given for the foundation of this church.[2] We may guess, but so far as written evidence goes it remains no more than a guess, that the original church would be one of the erections in the reign of King David I, who in the 12th century so lavishly built churches and endowed monasteries that one of his royal successors was afterwards to call him "a sair sanct for the Croon".

Suggestions of a specific date in the 12th century are highly probable but are based on gifts of land to the Diocese of Glasgow and such territorial bequests cannot be admitted as proof of the existence of an actual church. In the 12th century the secular lordship of Largs was held by the powerful de Morville family. From them it passed in the female line to the Lords of Galloway and, again in the female line, to the Balliols. The evolution of the ecclesiastical parish is less clear but, whensoever erected, the Parish of Largs first appears in the record stretching southwards from the boundary with the Parish of Ennerkip and embracing not only Skelmorlie, Largs and Fairlie but also the Cumbraes and a large part of Kilbride.

It would seem that in the middle ages the little church of St Columba was not unaided in the spiritual provision for this extensive parish. There were besides the chapel of Southannan dedicated to St Inan, the chapel of Haylie and the dependent chapel of St Colm on the Greater Cumbrae.[3] To the north there was the chapel of St Fillan, and nearby the farm of Chapelyards with its holy St Fillan's well; while in the glen were to be found the chapel of Rylies and the farm of Chapelton hard by. Even Kelso, the old name for Brisbane and said to mean "house of prayer", may point to the existence in earlier times of yet another chapel in Brisbane Glen.[4]

The incumbent responsible for the religious oversight of the Parish of Largs resided adjacent to the ancient churchyard. Until the beginning of the present century the Old Manse stood in Manse Court off Main Street. It housed between 1560 and 1762 no less than sixteen successive ministers of the Reformed Church, but it stood there even before the Reformation, its date being no later than 1536.[5] From its small windows the rectors of Largs may have looked down on scenes about which the ancient documents afford only a very occasional glimpse. Yet from such dim and hazy beginnings the Church of Largs played a part in the growth and development of faith and national freedom.

Perhaps even in this remote period, as in modern times, the congregation courted neither undue publicity nor cheap notoriety but went with steady and unobtrusive faithfulness about the work of

Christ's Kingdom. Investigation into the early history of the church serves to underline the old saying, "Out of the world and into the Lairgs" for Largs would appear to have played only a very minor part in the activities of the Scottish Church in pre-Reformation days. From ancient records one can compile lengthy lists of rectors, vicars and churchmen associated with other parishes but, perhaps on account of its remoteness from the beaten track of early communications, there are only the scantiest of references to Largs and its Church. The list of ministers in the post-Reformation centuries since 1560 can be completed in some detail but it has proved impossible to trace the name of a single incumbent during the 250 years before the Reformation when Largs was attached to Paisley Abbey and for the still earlier centuries throughout which it formed an independent rectory the records have so far yielded only two names.

The earliest mention of Largs Church in ancient records was for long believed to be in a Papal Bull of the year 1265. But in 1253 one William de Kilkenni, Archdeacon of Coventry, a prominent clerical statesman and counsellor of King Henry III of England, was appointed rector of the Church of Largs.

William, whose name appears variously as Kilkenni, Kilkennie and Kilkenny, makes his first entrance on the page of written history in 1237, in which year he figures as "King's Clerk" to Henry III. In the following year he is Canon of Salisbury "with licence to hold plurality of benefices without cure of souls". Pluralism, the holding of two or more lucrative offices concurrently, was a common feature of the medieval church. The revenues amassed were by no means the exclusive property of those who held the offices. Some profit accrued to the patrons who made the appointments and to the popes who confirmed them, and in many cases little can have remained for the parochial duties attached to such offices. About a decade later Kilkenni appears again, this time as Archdeacon of Coventry and in 1252 he was further advanced with licence to hold two additional benefices. The next year a papal letter confirmed to him

"disposition to hold his archdeaconry and other benefices which he now holds in England, with licence to receive others, and indult to hold also the

Church of Largis in the Diocese of Glasgow, a prebend of Dublin, and the treasurership of Exeter".[6]

In 1254 Kilkenni succeeded to the vacant bishopric of Ely and on his consecration to that See – the mother cathedral of Coventry – he laid down his position as Chancellor. King Henry sent Kilkenni in 1256 to negotiate a treaty with Alphonso, King of Castile. He lived just long enough to complete his mission. The treaty was signed by him on 20th September and he died on the 22nd or 23rd of the same month. He was buried in Spain but his heart was conveyed to Ely and deposited in his own presbytery there. In the Cathedral of Ely there is what is considered to be a very fine effigy of Kilkenni between two of the pillars beside the high altar.

Unfortunately, there is no hint that Kilkenni did anything for Largs nor even the slightest suspicion that he ever set foot in the parish. Yet it is pleasant to read in the *Chronicle of Matthew Paris* this at least of the first known Rector of Largs,

"He had the character of a modest, faithful and well-learned man, skilled in the canon and civil law, handsome in person, and eloquent and prudent".

Early in the 14th century another Rector of Largs appears in the person of William de Lyndesay, of whom little more can be said than that he resigned in 1318. But before his resignation took effect an event had happened which put an end to the independent rectory of Largs and shrouded its ecclesiastical annals in impenetrable darkness for almost two and a half centuries.

With the defeat of the Balliols in the War of Independence, Largs passed into the hands of Walter the Steward, the son-in-law of King Robert I and the progenitor of the Stewart kings. On 13th January 1318, Walter gave

"for the salvation of my soul and that of my late wife Marjorie, and for the salvation of my predecessors as also for all the faithful dead ... to God and Saint James, Saint Mirinus and Saint Milburga of Paisley and the monks of the same ... in pure and perpetual alms, the Church of Largs, with all the tithes, obventions, oblations and fruits ... pertaining thereto",

the grant to become effective on the death, resignation or promotion of the then Rector, William de Lyndesay. It was quite usual in transactions of this kind for the life-rent of the priest in occupation

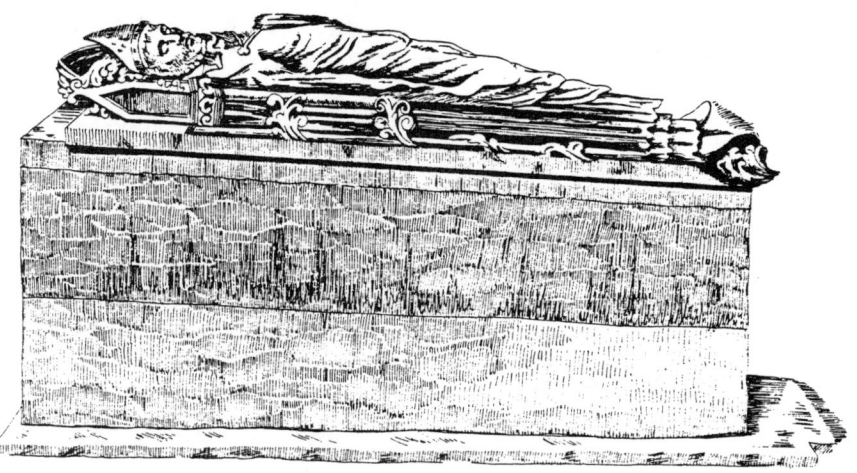

Effigy of William de Kilkenni, first known Rector of Largs, in Ely Cathedral.

to be safe-guarded but on this occasion it caused no delay. Lyndesay resigned on 3rd February, 1318 and the Abbey entered into full possession of Largs Church. [7]

To modern eyes the appropriation of country parish churches and their revenues by the great religious houses may seem strange and even iniquitous, but it was a common arrangement throughout the western Church; and in Scotland was part of a policy to compensate the monasteries which had been sorely impoverished by the wars with England. Not that country churches were always by this means ruined. The monasteries relieved the feudal superior of all responsibility for the management of his local churches and they usually undertook to make due provision for religious ordinances. Largs was an exception to this general rule. The original grant stipulated that the Abbey must place a vicar in the parish with a stipend of seventeen merks sterling, six acres of land and four wains of hay, and must also pay the bishop's fees and provide wax for the church lights. But about 1330 John, Bishop of Glasgow,

"out of consideration for the great damage sustained by the monastery of Paisley ... by reason of the war so long waged between the Kingdoms of England and Scotland and for the rebuilding of their church burnt in the said war" confirmed possession to Paisley Abbey of the Church of Largs and its dependent chapel on the Cumbrae without the customary obligation to settle a vicar in the parish so long as it was served by priests placed and removable at the monks' pleasure. The grant was again confirmed by Bishop William of Glasgow and, in July 1381, by a bull of Pope Clement VII, which emphasised that the church and chapel were not to be deprived of services nor the cure of souls neglected but were to be diligently served by secular presbyters.

Protected by these grants the Paisley monks could do as much, or as little, as they chose for the Parish of Largs. Possibly a minor brother would be sent down to administer the sacraments, exercise church discipline and exhort the faithful. Or perhaps a "secular presbyter", that is a priest not attached to any religious order, would be appointed to undertake the parochial duties. He would be paid a small stipend by the Abbey but would be without right to benefice or endowments, and would be styled "curate" or simply "chaplain". Priests of this low rank would be unlikely to appear as principals in records, and if they do appear – for example as witnesses – they may well be given no territorial designation. As a result, virtually nothing about the church of Largs can be found in the documents and for over 230 years there is no record of the name of a single vicar or chaplain associated with Largs.

Only once is this veil of obscurity lifted for a moment. In July 1319, Edward II of England made presentation to the Rectory of Largs of John de Hermyburgh, parson of Middleton-on-Tees [8]. It was one of several appointments made at this time by Edward, presumably because he claimed the patronage on the grounds of a vacancy in the See of Glasgow or of the forfeiture of the lay patron. Coming as it did five years after Bannockburn, the appointment must have been ineffective and can be dismissed as a vain gesture of defiance by a still enraged English sovereign.

Although only these two pre-Reformation Rectors are known – one an absentee and the other whose only known act was his demission of the charge – a few glimpses of the Church of Largs can be found. There is some evidence to suggest that it was considered quite a desirable living. William de Kilkenni was a confirmed pluralist, picking up lucrative benefices whenever they occurred; that he acquired one so remote as Largs seems to indicate that it was worth his while to do so. And certainly, the impoverished monks of Paisley wasted no time in taking over the Church. Within four days of the Steward's gift, the incumbent had resigned; and the subsequent appearance in documents of a William de Lyndesay, described as Archdeacon of St Andrews, may signify a hasty promotion to fulfil the conditions of the grant.

The revenue which the Abbey could hope to receive came in two kinds: teinds and rents. The teinds were the tithes payable to the Church by all and enforceable by law. Rents came from such of the "kirklands" as the monks chose not to work themselves. A rental-book of Paisley Abbey has survived and, although references to Largs are few, it shows how the monks administered their vast estates. The Abbey had a code of rules for its tenants but these amounted to little more than a standard of general behaviour that would not bring the Church into disrepute. Rents seem to have been reasonable and provided the tenant paid them regularly he could look forward to long-term occupancy and even to passing the land on in due course to his son.

Much of what was due to the Abbey was paid in kind and collecting it in an outlying place like Largs could be troublesome. Sometimes the Abbey appointed an agent to live at or near the church in order to gather in the goods and convey them to Paisley, giving him in return a piece of land on a very moderate rent. An even simpler method was to nominate a "tacksman of the teinds" who paid an annual sum to the Abbey and was then free to extract what he could, keeping any surplus for his own use. Both systems were in force at different times in Largs.

The rental-book notes that "the forty shilling land beside the Kirk of Largs" was let to

> "James Crafurd and Margaret Kelsoland, spouse of the said James, for two pounds annually, with horses and carts for collecting the teinds at the said land".

Another reference to James Crafurd indicates that his father had carried out this duty before him. In the mid 15th century the teinds were farmed out and trouble arose. A new Abbot of Paisley found that the Abbey was heavily in debt with most of its revenue in lay hands. He set himself to reform the financial position, obtaining permission from the Pope to revoke all existing arrangements. A certain laird named Robert Boyd of Tynwald had a lease of rents in Largs and tried to assert his claims by force. The Abbey appealed to the King who wrote:

> "James, be the grace of God Kyng of Scottis, till our lovid Robert Boid of Tynuald, gretynge: Foralsmekill as we ar informit tha yhe adres yhow to be at the Kyrk of Largyss on Friday nextocum, with a multitude of our liegess in feyre of were, in hurten and scath of our devote oratours the abbot and convent of Passelay, brekyn of our crya and offens of our maiestie, Our will is and straitly we charge yhow, gif it sua be, that ye desist tharof and mak na syk gaderin, under all the hiest payne and charge ye may inryne agane oure maiestie, and gif ye haif ochut aganes our said oratours, folond [i.e.summon] thame as law will. Gifwyn under our pryve scill at Edinburgh the xxiiij day of Aprile and of oure regne xiiij yhers".

In the ensuing lawsuit before the Commissary Court of the Dean and Chapter of Glasgow, the judgement on 23rd April was that

> "the claim of Robert Boyd, founded on the assedation to him by Sir Richard Bothuil, of the fruits of the church for the term of six years to be completed on the feasts of Saints Phillip and James in the year 1450 is valid and decreed to take effect; and that all other letters of assedation of the fruits of the church to the said Robert Boyd, by whomsoever made, are decreed to be invalid, and of no force or value".

The costs of the case were to be met equally by both parties to the dispute. Later, Patrick Shaw, vicar of Monktown and "farmer of the fruits of the churches of Largis and St Kennot" being in 1510 about to leave for Rome, appointed John Locard of Bare as his deputy until his return

> "to receive all debts due to him within the parishes of Largs and St Kennot of the fruits of the said churches remaining unpaid in the hands of the parishioners"

At times the Abbey received more than its due. On 5th January, 1403 John de Kelsou, son of the laird of Kelsouland, with the consent of his father, granted

> "to God and the blessed Virgin, Saints James and Mirinus of Paisley and the monks of the same, all his right and title to that proportion of land with its pertinents, commonly called Langlebank, lying in the barony of Cunninhame and shire of Are, between the ecclesiastical lands of the church of the parish of Largs on the west and the lands of Kelsouland in the east".

In the following year he added a half stone of wax from the lands of Kelsouland payable annually at the feast of St Mirinus. In March 1432, John Kelsow, dominus de Kelsowland, "for the safety of his soul and the soul of Christian Lewingston his spouse" granted to God and the saints and to the monks of Paisley, in free, pure and perpetual alms half a stone of wax at the feast of St Mirinus annually and gave the monks or their bailies power to destrain for non-payment. Interestingly enough, the rental-book notes "ye annual of kelsoland in ye largis zerly I stane of wax".

The place that the church held in the life of the community is illustrated by two legal papers. The church was a conspicuous and convenient building in which to meet to transact business. In the Charters of the Royal Burgh of Ayr there is an instrument:

> "... by Janet of Cairns, lady of one part of Busby, and John of Fergushill lord of the same, granting to Thomas Scott of Baillieland, for his service thankfully rendered, the lands of Hayandhouth and Atkyn's Croft, in the barony of Largs and the shire of Ayr: To hold of the granters in fee and heritage, for the yearly payment of sixteen pennies money of Scotland for Hayandhouth, and for Atkyn's Croft six pennies of the same money. Dated at the Parish Church of Largs, 20th July 1433".

And in 1538 the Burgh Charters and Writs of Irvine show that the Burgh of Irvine had complained to the King that its trading privileges were being infringed by merchants, chapmen and others who were setting up markets every Sunday at various parish churches, including Largs, to sell

> "hyde, woll, skynnis, claith, meill, malt, fische, flesche and ...
> all maner of small marchandice and cramry ware".

It follows that the local population must have been sufficiently numerous and sufficiently affluent to attract these travelling salesmen.

In the later medieval period most churches had a parish clerk. He was paid to act as assistant to the priest: his duties would include keeping the church clean and in good order; caring for vestments and furnishing; serving the priest at the altar; leading the responses and touring the parish weekly with holy water for the sick and dying. The office had a certain prestige and in country districts the parish clerk was often a member of the landed classes who accepted the emoluments and delegated the duties. In 1555 and again in 1559 John Montgomery of Flat is described as Parish Clerk of Largs.

As time passed, the authority of the Catholic Church declined. Ayrshire was in a sense the cradle of Scottish independence. It was also to the fore in pioneering the Scottish Reformation. In 1494 about thirty leading gentlemen of Ayrshire were put on trial as followers of John Wyclif. They were among the first Scottish protesters against the shortcomings of the Church. The need for some reform became widely recognised and as the 16th century progressed the Church made belated efforts to rectify some of the undeniable abuses of its power and wealth. But it was too late for internal reform to dam the flood of criticism. Iconoclastic mobs rioted in the wake of John Knox and other preachers, but on the whole the Protestants took over in Scotland with less hostility than in almost any other European country and by 1560 the Scottish Reformation was a *fait accompli*.

The Reformed Church was determined to encourage and educate the laity to participate in its control. This, it was hoped, would ensure adequate pastoral care in the individual parishes and would act as a safeguard against resumption of the abuses that had brought down the Roman Church. Nevertheless, zealous Reformers were speedily to discover that it is one thing to pull down, but quite another to build up. Church buildings might be available for congregations of the new persuasion; manses might pass to Protestant incumbents; but the dearth of ministers was to be a major problem of the Reformed Church for much longer than its first generation.

The Roman Church had dispersed the revenues of the Parish Churches to the larger religious houses whose property at the Reformation had generally fallen as secular lordships into the hands of the nobility. As a result, the shortage of clergymen was due not only to the limited number of men qualified for the ministry, but also the lack of funds to employ greater numbers.

The situation was partly met by the employment of readers, who appear to have been of two classes. Those of somewhat higher educational standing were designated "exhorters" and were permitted to deliver addresses. Those of the lower grade were simply "readers" whose main duty was to read "distinctly" the Common Prayers and the Scriptures. All were expected to teach the younger children.

Readers were sometimes junior clergy of the Roman Church, who for varying reasons were prepared to embrace the newer faith; others were laymen with some pretensions to higher education according to the standards of the time. The office of exhorter was phased out at an early date: some being promoted to be ministers and others being reduced to the lower, and since the need for economy was pressing, less remunerative status of readers. After 1573 every parish was supposed to be supervised by a minister. He might be in charge of several parishes and would be assisted by readers as helpers in each of the separate churches. These readers can perhaps be seen as the common ancestors of the Assistant Minister, the Session Clerk and the Parochial Schoolmaster of subsequent years.

DAVID NEIL

Precisely how the Reformation came to Largs is not known. In such a time of transition and with such a shortage of ministers, it is not surprising that the comparatively obscure Church of Largs was for many years without an ordained incumbent and that it fell to David Neil, Reader and Notary, to bridge the gap between the old Church and the new as the first Protestant in charge of the Church and Parish of Largs.

In the 16th century, the Notary Public was quite an important figure. He was a secular official who "noted" carefully details of land or property transactions so that authenticated evidence could be produced if any dispute arose later. It was not uncommon to find minor priests acting also as notaries and David Neil fitted into both roles.

The first incumbent of Largs Church was one of those who came over from the Roman communion, for he is described in 1556 as "curat" of Monkton. But before this time he appears as a Notary Public. In the Protocol Book of Sir John Crawford, the case book of a prominent west country Notary, the entry under 1548:

"Instrument narrating that David Neyll, chaplain and notary as procurator for the laird of Montfod, protested that Eleyng Bowman the relict of umquhill William Bwinteyng was not tenant to the said Laird of the ten shilling land of Skawart as alleged to the Laird. Done in Montfod's town, 14th day of February, 1540".

The lands of Montfod are in the parish of Ardrossan. At least one notarial instrument with a more local connection appears over Neil's hand. In it certain lands are conveyed in 1552 to John Kelso of Over Kelsoland, which is the older name for Brisbane. In other documents Neil is mentioned in 1554 as "Notary Public at Air".

Our concern, however, is less with the Notary than with the Chaplain. Neil is described as Reader in 1563 and again in 1567. He appears as Chaplain at Renfrew in 1575 but by 1576 he is again designated "Reidare at Largs". Plainly he was a man of some standing, and presumably he continued his notarial business to eke out the pittance paid by the Church for his services.

The more ancient ecclesiastical centre of the Parish is still clearly recognised in 1564 in an entry in the Accounts of the Lord High Treasurer specifying the Channon Lands of Largs under the familiar names of Baillielands, Harplaw, Rylies, Kilburn and Turgill.

In 1564 there would be sent down to David Neil two service books, the use of which would thereafter be obligatory to ministers, exhorters and readers. They were the Book of Common Order, to be for many generations the basis for the conduct of public worship, and the Psalm Book based on the versification of Sternhold and Hopkins which was for long to be the medium of congregational praise. They would be welcome enough to those who had received little training in the work of the ministry. As for the worshippers, those who absented themselves from the Sunday diets of worship had to pay a fine into the Poor Fund and it was the privilege of elders and deacons that they were "mulcted" of a much heavier fine if they failed to set a proper example by attending both the Sunday and weekday preachings.

It was during Neil's time at Largs that, in 1567, the Church of the Reformation was recognised as the rightly established church of Scotland and from then onwards it supplied the spiritual needs of the country with an increasing adequacy and growing man-power.

Indeed, before Neil's day was quite over it had close on 300 ordained ministers and over 700 readers.

Though little is known of David Neil's readership at Largs it was contemporaneous with stirring events of State. Largs is directly associated with the chequered career of Mary, Queen of Scots. In 1563 she stayed overnight at Southannan, where the powerful family of Sempyll had both a residence and a chapel dedicated to St Inan. Later, when Argyle, Huntly and the Hamiltons united their strength to the Queen's support it was at Largs they held a Convention. David Neil, the Reader at the Kirk of Largs, may have been an interested listener in the crowd that heard the first reading of the Proclamation issued by the Largs Convention of Nobles. It ran,

> "The Proclaimation of Archibald, Earl of Argyle, Lieutenant of the Queen, which summons all lords, barons and the like, betwixt sixty and sixteen ... to muster on 10th August, with twenty days victuals, to assist him as expedient, or to be held as traitors. Under his signet and subscription. At the Largis. 28th July, 1568".

There is just one more random note from this period. Was the little village of Fairlie, even in those remote days, famed already for its boat building? Or does the following extract merely indicate that the fishing industry was thriving there so long ago? The Calendar of Deeds under the date 5th July, 1569 records,

> "David Fairlie, younger of that Ilk, on behalf of William Aikin in the Fairly (and Robert Cwnynghame, a burgess of Edinburgh, Cautioner) on one part: and George Strathachin, burgess of Abirdene (and David Kintra in Leyth, Cautioner) on the other part: indenture — (anent) ... a boat to be furnished by the said William and sent to Lochcarrang for the herring fishery".

Neil's was in one respect a curious ministry. He was for various spells in Largs and then serving for longer or shorter periods in other places ranging from Renfrew to Ayr and he is found again in association with at least two of his ordained successors at Largs in the capacity of "helper". There is a later reference to him in 1590 as "sometime Reader at Largs, now in-dweller in Ayr". There he may have enjoyed a few years of retirement before the latest appearance of his name – the rather sad entry in the Ayr Burgh Accounts for 1601/2, "David Neil's wife had her rates remitted".

ALEXANDER CALLENDAR

The first ordained minister of the Reformed Church in Largs was Alexander Callendar. He was translated from Killearn to the triple charge of Largs, Kilbride and Ardrossan in 1574. The emoluments of the charge at that time were given as: to Alexander Callendar, Minister, £133:6:8d and the Kirklands; to the Reader at Largs, the post then being vacant, £16 plus some part of the Kirklands; to John Maxwell, Reader at Kilbride £20 and to George Boys, Reader at Ardrossan, the whole vicarage.

During the incumbency of Alexander Callendar, opposing influences were steadily at work. Two enactments may be mentioned both of which would have their effects in Largs.

In October 1579, Parliament ordained that every gentleman worth 300 merks yearly should forthwith possess himself of a Bible and a Psalm Book for the better instruction of himself and his family. As a consequence of this, several of the larger landowners in the parish must soon have become better equipped to appreciate the ministrations of Alexander Callendar in the Old Kirk of the Largis. And still larger numbers would no doubt, in this seaboard parish, be similarly affected by the companion act that made the same purchase obligatory upon every substantial seaman and burgess worth £50 in goods or lands.

Then too, if lonely isolation had at first been the feeling of the Presbyterian churchmen of the Lairgs cut off as they were from like-minded worshippers on the other side of the hills, a step was taken that must have imparted a new sense of fellowship and solidarity to their Christian work and witness. For it was decreed that 50 church courts should be erected throughout Scotland with the name of Presbyteries, and the General Assembly of 1581 decreed that a beginning of this work be made by the immediate inauguration of 13 Presbyteries, one of which was to be the Presbytery of Irvine. Of this Presbytery, Largs was one of the constituent charges from 1581 to 1834.

On the constructive side, then, this new impetus to Bible reading and Psalm singing, along with participation in the work of a Presbytery, must have done much to advance the cause of Presbyterian worship and government among the faithful. On the other side, certain subversive tendencies have to be noted. Struggling for its place in an atmosphere of hostility and general intolerance it is perhaps not surprising that the new Church leaned towards austerity, and even harshness, in its exercise of discipline thus hardening any opposition it encountered and alienating many from the new faith. Other unsettling influences were at work. One of the common names of old Largs, which continued up to fairly recent times, was the surname Ewing. At least one former holder of the name can hardly have been a popular figure, for in the *Inventory of Craiggan Writs* under the year 1584 is a discharge to Robert Ewing "Factor and Uplifter of the teinds of the Kirk of Larges". There was widespread resistance to attempts by the Church to suppress "Papist" folklore ceremonies in connection with holy wells, bonfires and "superstitious pilgrimages". An even more ominous threat to the Church came when James VI persuaded his Parliament to place on the Statute Book what came to be known as "the Black Acts". By these he asserted the doctrine, always so hateful in Scotland, that the King was the head of the Church as well as of the State and the sovereign in person was empowered to appoint bishops and to fix meetings of the General Assembly: two encroachments on religious sentiment and privilege that were in the course of time to be resisted and, even in 1584, were seen to be aiming at the establishment of Episcopacy which took place a quarter of a century later in 1610.

These disorders in the affairs of Scotland were bound to have repercussions far from the seat of government, and that Alexander Callendar had troubles of his own in Largs appears from the following extracts from the Register of the Privy Council.

"Anent oure Soverane Lordis letters rasit at the instance ofAlexander Callendar, minister of Goddis word at the Kirk of Largis in Cunynghame, makand mentioun. That quhair in the moneth of Julii last bipast Andro Maister Sympill, without ony occasioun offerit be the said Alexander, maist cruellie wald haif schot him with ane pistoll upoun the grene of Largis, being gangand betuix David Boill and Mathow Montgomery, wer not the said Andro wes stayit of his wicket purpois be the said David Boyll; and thaireftir send the said Mathow Montgomery to the said Alexander, dischargeing him to cum in his way, under the pane of deid. And upoun the xxiii day of October last the said Andro Sympill continewing in his wickit and ungodlie mynd, come to the place of Sowthennane quhair the said Alexander presentlie dwellis, and with ane drawin swerd unawaris wald have slayne him, wer not be Goddis providence he wes stayed be Robert Huntar of Hunterstoun; lyke as the said Andro proceding in his formar impietie aganis conscience and justice, laitlie upoun the fyft day of November last bipast come, accumpaneit with thre or four personis, to the place of Sowthennane the yettis thairof being stekit, and violentlie and be force brak up the same yettis with greit sparris and jeistis, and without mercy wald have slayne the said Alexander wer not be Goddis providence David Fairlie of that Ilk, and Williame Craufurde of Drumsey come for his help and relief; quhairthrow he dar not repair in thay partis for administratioun of the word of God for feir of his lyff."

The entry continues to the effect that the said Andro Sympill failing to appear to answer the complaint is denounced a rebel and put to the horn; that is, proclaimed an outlaw by the blowing of three blasts upon a horn.[9] Five months later, on 23rd April, 1578, a further entry is found:

"The quhilk day Robert Grahame of Knockdoliane become actit and obleist cautionar and souirtie for Andro, Master of Sympill, that the said Andro be himself, nor nane that he may let, sall invade, molest, nor persew Alexander Callendar, minister, in tyme cuming, utherwayis nor be ordour of law and justice, under payne of fyve hundrith pundis".

Alexander Callendar remained minister of Largs until 1584. It can only be hoped that the later years of his ministry were less turbulent.

WILLIAM FULLERTON

The next on the list of incumbents[10] – and this ministry was a very short one – is William Fullerton, son of John Fullerton of Dreghorn, and Janet Houston. He succeeded to Largs in 1585, but demitted office the next year. Possibly he went direct to Kilmaurs, where he is known to have been minister in 1589. Then in 1590 he was inducted minister of Dreghorn and Perceton. Called before the Privy Council on 5th February, 1610, he appears to have been charged with illicit traffickings with a Roman priest. In spite of this misdemeanour he remained in the charge of Dreghorn until his death in 1620, when he left behind a son, James, who in later years was minister at Beith.

Apart from that bare outline, the only other thing known about William Fullerton is a detail concerning his father. The Privy Council Register for 1587 has an entry bearing that John Fullerton of Dreghorn was that year a defaulter in the matter of his taxes. Even though we were to visit the sins of the fathers upon the children, local blushes can still be spared for by this time his son had already left Largs for Kilmaurs. And, in any case, not even the Dreghorn parent's public humiliation could prevent the son going to that very parish as minister three short years afterwards.

WILLIAM COCK

William Fullerton's successor at Largs was William Cock, who was to inaugurate the first really lengthy ministry in the parish. Son of John Cock, Cok or Cuik, burgess of Perth, he is known to have married Marion Nasmyth, by whom he had a son also named William. William Cock served the parish for many years from 1586, continuing in office till at least 1625. There is only that bald record of his lengthy ministry, yet during his forty years or thereby, great events were happening in Scotland, both in Church and State, and not infrequently these events must have affected the Largs community and kirk.

Early in William Cock's ministry an event of some significance in the history of Largs Church took place. After the Reformation Lord Claud Hamilton, Commendator of Paisley Abbey, acquired the lands and revenues of the Paisley monks. Converted into a temporal lordship, they were bestowed on him and his heirs under the title of Lord Paisley. The charter confirming this, dated 22nd March 1591/2, provided for the erection of a rectory in each of the churches formerly appropriated to the Abbey and for the payment of a stipend to the minister of each church.[11] This finally revoked the 14th century deed of gift and re-established the independence of the Church of Largs.

It was a time when the heavy hand of Church discipline came down without mercy, and without respect of persons, on gentle and simple alike. Had the Church records of the day survived we might well have read of a proud landowner on one page and a humble fisherman on another being made to stand on three successive Sundays at the door of the kirk, clad in sackcloth and barefooted, bearing a paper crown inscribed with the name of his dire offence; then moving indoors to stand thus before the pulpit for public rebuke during the sermon before resuming his place at the door as a spectacle for the skailing kirk.

But though the Kirk Session minute-book of William Cock's time has perished, other sources provide at least one example in Largs of the harsh measures that discipline sometimes involved. It is a case of excommunication and in these days that was no light affair. It meant not only exclusion from the privileges of the Church itself but also a very real measure of social ostracism for the offender, and woe betide the unhappy third party who sought any means of contact with the poor creature who was thus without the pale. In 1603 we find Robert, Lord Sempill forced to provide security

"for Robt Montgomerie, Thos Montgomerie, Robert Ewing, John Boyd, younger, and Robert Brown, his servants and tenants in Southannan, two hundred merks each, not to reset or intercommune with William Montgomery, elder, in the isle of Little Cumrey, nor with his family ... conform to the charge given to them 1st Feby, 1603. Written before Johnne King and Johnne Harper, indwellers in Largis".

By such means even his closest friends were dared to do any small turn to relieve the tedium and isolation of the unfortunate William until he had made full satisfaction to the Church authorities.

And what of the early elders under this Presbyterian system of Church government? It seems hardly open to doubt that a primary duty on the Sabbath was to keep an eagle eye on the plate. Probably at Largs, as elsewhere, it was ordained that they should be at the doors before service commenced "so as to keep ye people from raming past without putting anything in ye box": as Robert Louis Stevenson put it "sentinels over the brazen heap". Offerings went towards such Poor Relief as there was, for from the beginning the Reformed Church had a lasting responsibility for the poor. An Act of 1589 authorised Kirk Sessions to appoint officers to deal with idle beggars and vagabonds, and five years later they were empowered to try to deal with drunkards. On the other hand, while thus getting rid of habitual nuisances, they could issue badges to favoured mendicants to beg throughout their own parishes. To William Cock's elders, whoever they may have been, fell also the duty of "delating" absentees from public worship. We can imagine the elder from the North End and the South End respectively keeping a keen look-out for the tenants of Fardens and Southannan and having them duly fined by the Session if their attendance fell short of the required standard.

The Union of the Crowns of 1603 brought an obviously growing attempt at Episcopal domination. The establishment of Episcopacy over the Church of Scotland in 1610; the introduction of Anglican church festivals in 1617 and the Five Articles of Perth in the following year contributed to unrest which was to last throughout the first Episcopacy from 1610 to 1638 and then give place to the stirring half century of the Scottish Covenanters.

Since we are without information about William Cock's personality we know nothing of his reactions to the changing order in the Church. He would benefit from an Act of 1606 which provided that there should be assigned to the minister of each parish "16 soumes of grass". A soume of grass in these days would pasture ten sheep or one cow for a whole year, and this acreage was to be provided from the kirklands nearest to the church. Since the manse stood then in what is now named Manse Court, off Main Street, this may be taken as the origin of the Glebe of Largs on the South Kirklands, which were divided by the Noddle Water from the North Kirklands. So that William Cock was probably the first of the farming ministers of Largs: a race now long extinct. The General Assembly of 1615 cut down the praise of the Church to only twelve common tunes for the Psalms, a step which throughout Scotland must have seriously impoverished public worship.

William Cock was perhaps pleased when one of his own parishioners, John Frazer of Knock, was appointed in 1627 as one of the Scottish Commissioners for the Improvement of Stipends. Yet any expectation he may have indulged of preferential treatment was to be sadly disappointed since the long overdue improvement did not materialise until the days of his successor at Largs.

During William Cock's ministry the life of the Scottish nation was not without excitement. The power of Spain was the terror of Western Europe and the destruction of the Spanish Armada was not without its touch of local colour for, if tradition may be trusted, one of the galleons sank off Portencross.[12]

But Spain defeated, was not yet Spain done with. Just four years later on 27th December 1592, excitement must have run high among those who plied their fishing boats between Largs and the Cumbrae. For nothing less than a plot against King James VI was afoot and a conspirator had been arrested as he was about to set sail from Fairlie Roads. His belongings were searched, and concealed in the sleeves of a shirt were found letters appealing to Spain for an invasion of Scotland to depose the King and restore the Catholic Church. Among the papers were empty schedules signed by the Earls of Huntly, Errol and Angus and from these the affair has come to be known in history as the "Spanish Blanks".[13] The plotter was carried off to Edinburgh under a strong military guard, leaving sensation behind. It was said that the alert ministers of the locality helped to unravel this conspiracy of the rebel lords: William Cock may, or may not, have had a hand in the incident.

At this time Scotland enjoyed little internal peace. Representations were made to the King concerning the spiritual condition of the country. And little wonder. Duels were fought in kirk and kirkyard and side by side with overcrowded churches, was a deplorably low standard of morals. But slowly and surely the insularity of Largs with all its disadvantages was being broken down. The Plantation of Ulster was begun in 1607. Ayrshire was prominently represented in this venture and in later years Largs was to recruit ministers out of the Presbyterian communities of Northern Ireland.

In the first half-century of the Reformed Church, parochial education lagged far behind the high ideals of John Knox. It was to be many long years before there was a school in every parish. Nevertheless, in this respect Largs was somewhat in advance of many parishes and had its local teacher even before the end of the 16th century. The earliest reference traced occurs in a contract between a Boyle and a Cunningham of Skelmorlie; subscribed by them on 12th June 1595, at the Kirktown of Largs before certain witnesses, one of whom is designated "James Bennet, Schoolmaster of Largis". Another schoolmaster, Thomas Mure, is similarly ascertained to have succeeded some time before 1605, so that perhaps Bennet was an old man who had already served for some time in 1595. Be that as it may, Largs anticipated the School Act of 1616, that decreed a school should be set up in every parish, providing some sort of education at a date comparatively soon after the Reformation. These notes on local education may be rounded off at a higher level by stating that one of the Largs gentlemen of the day, John Boyle of Kelburn, a Judge of the Court of Session, was twice Lord Rector of Glasgow University.

Among the landed families, the long-standing vendetta of the Cunninghams and Montgomeries was carried, not for the first time, to murder. Somewhere about 1591 Alexander Cunningham, Commendator of Kilwinning Abbey, was struck dead at his own door by Robert Montgomerie, the father of the later Sir Robert Montgomerie who was to erect the Skelmorlie Aisle. In 1595 the Brisbanes of Bishopton consolidated their position as the leading landowners of the parish. Prior to 1400 they had acquired Killincraig and Gogo. Gradually they added Tourgill, Harplaw, Rylies and the Channons, along with the lands of Halie. Their estates also included Nether Kelsoland, Flatt and Hangingheugh and in 1595 the whole was erected into the Barony of Gogoside and the town into a Burgh of Barony under the name of Newtown of Gogo.[14]

But there seem to have been certain lawless tendencies among the citizens of the new burgh. The records of the Privy Council refer in 1602 to a charge that

"a nowmer of wretchit catives and unworthie personis of the townis of Glasgow, Renfrew, Dumbarton, the Largis, Irwin and Ayr ... preferring their unlawful gain to a gude conscience"

had permitted goods to be transported for the use of rebels in Ireland. It ends by summoning the Provosts and Bailies of these particular "townis" to appear and answer the charge. That the seafaring folk of Largs had less interest in the Irish rebels than in the pickings to be derived from illicit trading with them may not unfairly be deduced from the notoriety they enjoyed a century and a half later as smugglers. But as if to compensate for the restrictions put on local cupidity in 1602 in the matter of running goods to Ireland, Largs was in 1627 appointed, along with Irvine, a recognised port of traffic with that country.

A few local names of the 17th century, noted from various sources, may be of interest: Wm Small in Dykes; Robert Russell in Mylnerig; Patrick Montgomerie in Blackhouse and Jonathon Scott there; William Holme, Thos Brown, and John Kelso in St Phillan's Well; David Pharie and Robt Jamie in Largs; Johne Aiken, merchant in Largs; David Or in Largs and John Sinclair; Alex Jamieson fiar in Hale; David Kelso of that Ilk and his brother Henry in Flatt; John and William Montgomerie, rebels; Archd and Jas Connell, notaries; along with Edward and John Simpson, John Clark, Robt Fairlie, Robt McLaine, Walter Fairlie, Alex and David Blackburne, George Boyd, John Or, David Aickine, and John Hude, all in Fairlie; with Robt Forrest, forester there; David Hutcheon at Southannan and John Kyle in Fairlie Mylne.

Passing from vague names to the clearer light of contemporary life, there is a curious sidelight on the times of the Rev. William Cock. The troops of King James being on an expedition to the Western Isles in the summer of 1608, a royal edict went out in the following terms:

> "The fencibles being to meet at Yla on 1st July necessar it is that provision be maid of viveris for their intertainment during their imployment in that service ... there is order therefore to charge the magistrates at Kirkcudbright, Wigtoun, Ayr, Renfrew, Dumbarton, Irwing, Saltcoats, Largis, and other townis of the west coast to have vessels provided with biscuit, wine, ale, beer and other victuals, ready to follow the army, and to sell same for competent prices".

This was the little world of Largs about 1600 where William Cock fulfilled his long ministry. It is not known precisely when his incumbency terminated, but by 1631 another – and it is to be feared a less worthy – man was occupying his pulpit.

THOMAS CRAIG

The date of the admission of William Cock's successor is not known. All that can be said with certainty is that Thomas Craig was minister of Largs by 12th May, 1631. His degree of Master of Arts had been conferred by the University of Glasgow in 1617 and he had been on the "Exercise" in that city in 1620. Since the Exercise was really the forerunner of the Presbytery it may be assumed that Craig was at first a minister in or around Glasgow and at a later date was translated to Largs. In 1632 he contributed towards the inauguration of the library in Glasgow University. Hardly any more authentic details seem to be available regarding him but perhaps this is not even to be regretted since it was deposition that brought his ministry to an untimely end about 1640.

As minister of Largs Thomas Craig did not have to serve, as some of his predecessors had, the whole of Ardrossan and Kilbride parishes as well, although for some time longer the parish of Largs embraced Southannan, Whiteside and Crosbie. Yet although the duties were somewhat lightened, the stipend had become better having participated in the increase effected throughout the Church about 1633, after some sixteen years of negotiation with unwilling landowners. Nevertheless Craig would have to part with a portion of his increased stipend; for in 1633, in obedience to an enactment of King Charles I, Scottish ministers were obliged to furnish themselves with a white Anglican surplice in place of the black scholar's gown worn by the clergy of the Reformed Church.

At this period the kirk bell would be rung three times each Sabbath morning: first at seven o'clock to warn the parishioners to prepare for worship; again at eight for the earlier part of public worship taken by the Reader who would read the prayers and long portions of the Scriptures; finally when the third bell ceased at nine o'clock the minister himself would enter the pulpit during the singing of a psalm and proceed with his part of the service which included the sermon.

It was during Craig's ministry that, in 1636, there was erected alongside the church the Skelmorlie Aisle, which stands yet in its strength and beauty though the parent edifice has long since disappeared. In the following three years the Aisle was embellished with the paintings that can still be seen on the ceiling, and further enhanced by the erection of the monument whereby Largs shares with Kilmaurs and Dunlop the only good specimens of the art of the monumental sculptor of that day now to be found in Ayrshire.

But while the Skelmorlie Aisle was being built and decorated much was happening in Scotland and in Largs. Charles I was born in Scotland; was baptised by a Presbyterian minister and educated by Presbyterian tutors but he grew up unable to understand either his northern kingdom or its religious ideas. The repercussions of his blundering insistence on introducing Archbishop Laud's Liturgy into the Scottish Church were to be disastrous. It may have been true, as his party insisted, that in Scotland "preachers, readers and ignorant schoolmasters prayed so ignorantly as to be a shame to all religion". It cannot, however, be too clearly stated that the objection in Scotland was not so much to formal prayers as to the imposition of the unpopular liturgy by royal edict instead of by agreement of the General Assembly. And besides asserting that it was unlawfully brought in, there were those who complained of "Popish" tendencies in the orders of service.

But if the King, obstinate and fanatical, was determined to have his way in the matter of public worship, his Scottish subjects were equally determined to have none of it. Their resistance to Laud's Liturgy is now a part of our general history and the riot in St Giles with its familiar "Jenny Geddes" embellishments is well known. What far fewer know is that on the day appointed for the introduction of the new Service Book, the clergyman at Largs, too, had a rough time. He commenced to read from the obnoxious pages and got only so far as the words, "This is my rest, here will I stay, for I do like it well". At that, an old woman in the congregation cried out, "An' it will be a great peety if ye dae onythin' o' the kind". Thereupon, two brothers Morrice, of the Killincraig, rose up from their place in the kirk and unceremoniously bundled the offending preacher out of the pulpit.[15]

Up and down the land petitions were signed against the new Service Book. That from "the gentlemen and remnant people of the Largis" was signed by:

"David Boyll, feir of Kelburne; Skelmorlie; John Frazer of Knok; J Fraser; J Crawford; Patrick Schaw of Kelsoland; and Archibald Kelso in Flatt"

who were heritors; as well as by the elders:

"Henrie Wilsone; Williame Henrie; Robert Ewing; Johne Scott; George Thomesone; Colene Grant; Patrick Craufuerd; Johne Fraser and Johne Patersone, Clerk to the Sessione of Largis".

The minister did not sign, although John Paterson did and he is known to have been Reader, or Assistant Minister, as well as Session Clerk.

There is no evidence that Thomas Craig himself officiated on the day that the zealous opposition of the two Killincraig stalwarts bore the preacher out of the church, but it seems more than likely that such was the case. For one thing, Craig was plainly on anything but good terms with the leaders of the Presbyterian party. Robert Baillie notes in his Journal for 1637,

"promised to write to Mr Thos. Craig that it was our desire he should be earnest with old Skelmorlie to carrie their supplication"

which suggests that Craig was not very willing to bring pressure on his leading landowner to convey the Largs petition to the proper authorities. It may also be significant that Craig was no longer minister at Largs a year or two later, and it is likely that some tendency on his part to be indulgent towards prelacy may have brought about the deposition already mentioned and have given point to the comment of the severely Presbyterian Baillie – one of the "Men of the Covenant" – that,

"Mr Thos. Craig is like to prove such a villain, that he is worthie of more punishment than deposition".

Calling Baillie one of the Men of the Covenant introduces that great event in Scottish history, the signing of the National Covenant at Greyfriars Kirk in 1638. It was the natural sequel of the King's refusal to pay heed to the petitions then pouring in from all over Scotland. "We know no other bonds between a King and his subjects", the petitioners declared, "than those of religion and the laws; and if these are broken, men's lives are not dear to them." Ayrshire was prominent in signing the Covenant; her earls of Loudon, Cassilis and Eglinton appending their names to the manifesto. And when in the same year the General Assembly defied the King by restoring Presbyterianism and abjuring Prelacy, the Covenanters' call to arms was answered by Eglinton "with the whole countryside at his back". Ministers were ordered to read the Covenant from

Skelmorlie Aisle was a small chapel added on the north side of the Church to house the burial place of the Montgomeries of Skelmorlie. A fragment of the wall of the original Church can be seen in the foreground. It was left intact when the Church was demolished as it carried a memorial, now much eroded, to the Boyles of Kelburn.

their pulpits and some were deposed for refusing to comply with the injunction. It was perhaps his failure to carry out this order of the supreme court of the Church that brought about Thomas Craig's dismissal, an event which cannot have been later than 1640.

Before passing to another ministry, a random note from the period may throw some light on the state of the fishing industry around Largs three hundred years ago. It is to the effect that the Cannon Lands of the old Diocese of Glasgow, within the parish of Largs, were held by Lord Boyle for an annual payment, among other things, of "six thousand Red Herrings".

WILLIAM SMITH

John Paterson is known to have been Reader at Largs in 1634 and 1637 but it was not he who succeeded Thomas Craig as minister.

The next incumbent was William Smith, whose ministry was to be as eventful as it was brief. Like his predecessor, a Master of Arts of Glasgow University, he graduated there in 1639 and as a young man was schoolmaster at Kilwinning in 1641. His ministry at Largs began in 1644, on the very eve of momentous happenings, both in Scotland and in his own parish. Across the border the troubles of King Charles had entered upon a new phase, and war had broken out between the Parliamentary party and the Royalists. An alliance between the ill-fated monarch's enemies in England and his ill-used Presbyterian subjects in Scotland was natural. In 1643, the year before William Smith arrived in Largs, these two parties had come together and sworn the Solemn League and Covenant, binding all loyal Presbyterians to fight for the extirpation of popery and prelacy. Thus William Smith began his work at Largs at a time when the affairs of Scotland, in both kirk and state, were practically in the hands of the Covenanting leaders; headed by the Duke of Argyll, with Montrose as general of the Royalist forces.

Unfortunately, we have no record to indicate how this latest Covenant was received in Largs. But unless the parish was very different from others whose attitude to the Covenant has been chronicled, we can conclude that doctrinal knowledge and spiritual enthusiasm were on a high enough level for the great majority of the people to accept the Covenant with a real degree of understanding.

Civil war raged in England, and in Scotland Montrose went his all-conquering way against the forces of the Church, winning the Battle of Kilsyth in 1645. Whatever opposition there may have been to the King in Largs, it is clear that Montrose was not without his supporters in the parish. Frazer of Knock, for example, is listed among the western "malignants" who declared for Montrose and the King, and one Alex Beith was involved with him in the charge.

Presbyteries were enjoined to proceed against all who had taken protection from Montrose. Thus, the Presbytery of Irvine felt it incumbent on them to deal with the Laird of Knock, who, like many more who thought Kilsyth sealed the fate of the Covenanting party, had waited upon the victor at Glasgow to congratulate him and to profess attachment to the King. The wily Frazer contrived to evade these ecclesiastical proceedings and to escape sentence by taking ship for Ireland. Had he waited seven months longer before coming out for Montrose he might have remained in Largs, for the Royalist forces under Montrose were routed by Leslie at Philiphaugh in 1645.

During the ministry of William Smith the Presbytery of Irvine became seriously exercised about the inadequacy and inconvenience of the little parish church. Accordingly, on 27th July 1647, certain commissioners from the Presbytery to the General Assembly were appointed "to deal with my Lord Abbercorne for the division of the paroch of Larges".[16]

After preliminary investigation, on 7th December
> "the Presbiterie considering the great necessitie of erecting a new kirk within the paroch of Larges, namely, the multitud of the communicants, exceeding the number of 2,000; the largeness of the boundes of the paroch, extending to full ten myles of length; the incapacitie of the present place of meiting not being able to containe the half of the people; and the great hazard that great many of the people is in by coming to the present kirk by reason of the water callit Gogo that runs throw the midst of the paroch quhilk after raining becomes almost impassable even to horses and it runneth with sick violence that ther is no possibilitie to get a bridge upon it; upon this and the like considerations the Presbyterie does conclude the necessitie of a division of the paroch".

Commissioners were appointed
> "to meit this day fourteen dayes at Southannan with the heritours of the paroch to represent to them the necessitie of a division, and to deile with them for their concurrence and report their diligence".

On 18th January, 1648 the Presbytery
> "does think it necessarie that there be a present perambulation of that paroch whereunto the whole gentlemen, Kelburn only being exceptit, has condescendit".

Again commissioners were named to
> "be at the pains to visit the said paroch upon Thursday come eight days for finding out the place most convenient for situation of a new kirk and to report their diligence".

In due course the committee reported that the site
> "suld be upon the south syd of the water of Gogo, within the Laird of Fairlie his land upon ane parcel of grund callit Sandflatten"

and it was decided that Mr John Nevay
> "sall give in ane supplication to the Lords Commissioners for the Plantation of Kirks".

Annexed to the familiar reasons for the division was a new argument,
> "the state of the paroch, being now destitut of a minister, is such, partlie because of the aforesaid reasons, and partlie because of the stubborness of many of the people in it, that the Presbiterie does almost despair of getting any honest man who will undergo such a burthen except the paroch be devydid"

Two points in the foregoing extract can be noted. We read of "the paroch being now destitut of a minister" which indicates that while the court was busied with these perambulations, the young minister of Largs had already died. The other point is the reference to John Nevay as the Presbytery's commissioner to prosecute the Largs matter before the Edinburgh authorities. As the minister of Loudon, Newmilns, Nevay was a prominent Covenanting leader, a scholar, and something of a poet. He was one of four ministers entrusted by the General Assembly of 1647 with the final revision of the Rous version of the metrical Psalms, which was to receive Assembly authorisation in 1650. To each of the others were apportioned forty of the Psalms and the last thirty – numbers 121 to 150 – were allotted to Nevay. So that while the minister of Loudon was meditating his retouching of "I to the hills will lift mine eyes", he was in that same year of 1647 faithfully perambulating the Lairgs with his co-Presbyters and lifting his eyes to its background of hills.

But to return to the parish and the slow progess of negotiations for its division. The lumbering machinery of "Presbiterie" was soon to be brought to a standstill by a more sinister form of visitation. The Presbytery minutes of 29th June 1647, bear that
> "the referrs that concern the Larges are continued because of the seikness there".

Later, in September occurs a further note,
> "the Presbiterie laying to heart the lamentable and calamitous condition of the paroch of Larges, partly by reason of the hand of God that is lying heavy upon them, and partly by reason of the removal of their minister by death, think it is expedient that Mr William Lindsay be sent to visit them, and to take notice of their desires, and to enquire ane overture of themselves how they may be gotten helpit and supplied".

Not only were ordinances, it would appear, totally suspended in the distressed parish but the next month the Laird of Bishoptoun remonstrated on the calamitous conditions, asserting that,
> "if it were not tymeously removit and helpit the people wald be forcit to break out athort the countrie".

That Bishoptoun did not overstate the case may be inferred from the persistent local tradition that many of the inhabitants did indeed flee the town and build for themselves a colony of huts or rude temporary dwellings in the vicinity of Outerwards. The phrase "helpit and supplied" seems to have envisaged material as well as spiritual aid, for the Presbytery was moved to a signal act of compassion and collections on behalf of the stricken Largs were taken in Newmylnes, Irwin, Kilmaurs, Stewartoune, Kilwinning, Perston, Kilbirnie, Dreghorne, Dalry and Ardrossan.

Following upon the ruinous pestilence, the impoverished state of the parish put a full stop to negotiations for the new kirk. Compromise ensued. The southermost lands of Southannan and Corsbie were disjoined from Largs about 1650 and annexed to Kilbryd; and the old kirk of Largs, condemned and inadequate, was destined nevertheless to serve the parish as best it might for nearly two centuries longer. Further, the wide area of the parish was to remain intact until the building of the Fairlie Chapel of Ease in 1833.

The Presbytery's plans for the parish were halted by the continued devastations of the pestilence, but before that the Rev. William Smith had himself succumbed to its attack. He contracted the disease whilst faithfully visiting his afflicted parishioners, in September 1647. That a career of real promise was thus cut short may be deduced from the following memoir, contributed to Wodrow's *Analecta* by the Rev. Mr Stirling, minister of Barony Church, Glasgow:

> "Mr William Smith ... who was my father's schoolmaster at Irwine, was ordained Minister of Largs, as I suppose. He was a choice man for piety, and had an excellent popular gift of preaching, most taking with the people. He was with Mr James Glendinning at his Communion in Kilbarchan. My dear mother told me she heard Mr William Smith preach notably at that Communion upon these words, Ezek. xx. 37. She told me she and many others were much refreshed with what he delivered at that time. She told me some of his most choice and excellent notes. She thought he had much of God and of heaven even in his very face and countenance, so that she thought he could not be long out of heaven; and it fell out most exactly to be so; for about fourteen or twenty dayes after, that worthy and most excellent Mr Smith was removed by death. For when my mother went to Paisley, on a week-day, to hear Mr Dunlop preach, when she came to the Church-yard of Paisley, the Elder that collected that day told her that Mr

Dunlop was gone away to Largs to be at Mr Smith's burial. He was thought to be far above his brother Mr Hugh, who also was a godly and worthy Minister.

Mr William Smith was once at a Communion Table, I do not certainly know whether it was at Largs or elsewhere, and he saw all the people generally in a most sweet, pleasant, melting, and desireable frame. He cried out, 'Welcome, welcome, Holy Ghost, doun amongst us!' Mr Smith was somewhat lame in some of his feet."

William Smith was about 28 years of age at the time of his death and it was noted that

"being ane young man unmarried he had no cowes, cattel, nor vther moveable guidis, except allenerlie certaine small insycht and plenishing of his chalmers, with his buikis and abuilzements of his body".

By his own wish William Smith was buried in the little valley where a burn runs down to join the Noddle Water close by the farmhouse of Middleton where he died. According to tradition, he said on his deathbed regarding the place he had chosen for his burial, that so long as the two adjacent holly trees did not meet over his grave the plague would never again visit his parish. This dying prophecy has been handed down in local lore and has given his burial place its name "The Prophet's Grave".

JAMES GLENDINNING

The vacancy after William Smith's death lasted for more than a year, and during it at least one Ayrshire man with Largs connections appeared in national history. In September, 1648, some of the inhabitants of the western shires raised a force of armed men, mostly extreme Covenanters, who marched on Edinburgh to set up a new government there. Their descent on the capital became known as "The Whiggamore Raid" and its only lasting consequence was to provide the name of "Whigs" for a rising political party. The leader of the Whiggamore Raid was Colonel Robert Montgomerie, son of the Earl of Eglinton and kinsman to Montgomerie of Skelmorlie.

Between the local devastation of the epidemic and the ecclesiastical strife that was so soon to engulf the nation, Largs had one ministry of comparative calm. William Smith died at the early age of 28; he was succeeded by a man already more than twice his age. James

Glendinning studied at St Leonard's College in St Andrews and graduated there soon after 1617. He went to Ulster, where he was minister of Coole or Carnmoney – a parish between Belfast and Carrickfergus – and a lecturer at Carrickfergus; so that he must have had some reputation as a scholar. It was said that he had "a great voice and vehement delivery" and that his preaching had a pronounced effect on the hearers. He became involved with a Revivalist movement that was "at first a great blessing to many" but later was strongly criticised for excesses that led many of his colleagues to regard him as mentally disturbed. This, no doubt combined with the increasingly difficult political situation in Ireland, caused him to return to Scotland, where, in spite of the condemnation of the Irish clergy, he was to have a long and apparently respected career.

By 1644 Glendinning was attached to the Presbytery of Paisley. He was never actually minister of Kilbarchan but deputised there frequently during the minister's ill-health and, after his death, took over responsibility for that parish, where he signed the Solemn League and Covenant in 1648. There was a proposal that he should be officially appointed minister, but for some reason this did not take place and it was Glendinning himself who recommended a minister named John Stirling to the Kirk Session. "Call this young man," he said, "for he is an old-headed and experienced Christian though he is but a young preacher". Following Stirling's induction to Kilbarchan James Glendinning, who must then have been in his mid-sixties, was placed temporarily at Largs in 1649.

After the execution in that same year of King Charles I, power passed into the hands of Cromwell and his Protectorate. The Scottish Covenanters secured the abolition of patronage by an Act of Parliament, and thus had the matter of nominating their ministers left to the elders of the Kirk. This, however, was but one of the many changes in regard to patronage, which was to be often abolished and often restored. It may well be that James Glendinning took a memorial service in the autumn of 1650 for John Montgomerie, Laird of Blackhouse, who had fallen on 2nd September fighting against Cromwell at the disastrous Battle of Dunbar.

The worship of the Church underwent notable changes at this period. In 1650 the old Scots Psalter gave place to the version of Francis Rous, drastically and frequently revised before its adoption into the Scottish Church. But, as then adopted, it has continued to do duty in three successive Parish Churches of Largs for almost three centuries and across nineteen ministries right up to the present day.

There were other important changes in public worship. The century old tradition of Presbyterian worship, bequeathed by the Scottish reformers, was debased by influences imported from the extreme Puritan party across the border. Such truly Scottish customs as the daily service; the offering of private prayer on entering the sanctuary; the use of forms of prayer; the regular reading of fixed portions of Scripture and the repetition of the Lord's Prayer: all these, and more, that had prevailed for a hundred years, were swept away by disciples of English independency as supposedly Anglican and Roman tendencies. And, by one of the ironies of history, the bleakness thus imported from the south has come to be hailed by many present day worshippers as the essentially Scottish type of service. Such a travesty of Church history might well make John Knox and the Fathers of the Scottish Reformation turn in their graves.

Under such alien influences the worship of the Church of Scotland sank lower and lower in the next 200 years. People went to Church to hear a sermon, rather than to worship God. Disorderliness in worship often led to disorderly conduct among the worshippers and even sometimes to disgraceful scenes within the Church itself.

It is not to be supposed that Largs was any better in this respect than other churches of the day. So let us, in imagination, enter Largs Church on any Sabbath in the 1650s. The praise led by the Precentor has been cut to a minimum to make room for two lectures and two sermons by Mr Glendinning for, at this time, the preachings are everything and the hours of service long by any standards. As the Rev. James holds forth for the third or fourth time, we may begin to feel decidedly drowsy. Perhaps we may become a little envious of the younger worshippers with inkhorn and exercise book busily taking notes of the sermon to be familiar with its various heads at the afternoon catechising or when it is made the subject of question and answer during the next week's schooling. If we become too somnolent a sudden vicious jab in the ribs may well make our nodding head rise bolt upright from our chest. It is the beadle prodding us back to attention with his duly authorised pole. This important functionary has other duties to perform to maintain order among the congregation. He must see to the ejection of "greeting bairns"; he must quell lusty urchins who run through the church "clattering and fighting in time of service"; and he must carefully observe the worshippers in order to report to the Kirk Session any who venture – in the absence of peppermints – to "take snuff in time of divine service".

Once the minister has finished with "Lastly", and "Finally", and "One word more" and has resumed his seat, the elders may well proceed to uplift a special collection for some worthy cause in addition to the ordinary door collection for the local poor. Its relevance to Largs may not be immediately obvious: for repairs to the harbour wall at Kirkcaldy, perhaps, or towards the ransom of ten Buckie fishermen carried off as slaves to some outlandish part of the world.

Imagination? Well, yes and no! Imagination so far as Largs is concerned, for all records of the period have vanished. Yet not wholly imagination, for the picture is compiled strictly from actual records surviving in other parishes.

During James Glendinning's ministry Largs perhaps lost some of its population, for there was a large new emigration to Ulster after Cromwell's settlement of Ireland in 1652. Fairlie, then a fishing village of only a few houses in the south end of the parish, had trading connections with Ireland, carrying over fish and cattle and bringing back butter and corn. Probably few local people, even among the lairds, would have thought of travelling to London at this time; but for any who cared to venture, the year 1658 bought luxury unheard of until then. A stagecoach began to make the journey from Edinburgh to London in not more than one week, except when snow or rain made the roads a little worse than usual and lengthened the journey.

Although nothing is known of James Glendinning's activities in Largs, his actions elsewhere indicate a great deal about his character.

His contemporaries admired his charitable works saying, "He gave very much to the poor, even to the straitening of himself and family". Francis Sempill of Beltrees, in an eulogistic poem addressed to Archbishop Leighton, cited Glendinning as the ideal of philanthropy. Sempill wrote to the Archbishop:

"We think ye do richt weil
To give the poor your winning,
In money, malt and meal;
We think ye do richt weil;
We never knew your peel
But auld Mr James Glendinning."

From Largs, Glendinning continued to take an interest in Kilbarchan and its young minister. John Stirling found his parish far from easy to handle. Several people appeared before the Kirk Session on charges of drunkenness, Sabbath breaking and "fechting and flyting". Eventually "to the great shame and confusion of the minister" there were no less than five cases of adultery. James Glendinning hastened to Kilbarchan to advise and encourage John Stirling, whose son afterwards contributed an account of the visit to Wodrow's *Analecta*. It shows that Glendinning adopted a very positive attitude towards the crisis, for James Stirling wrote:

"He came to see my father after these five adulterys broke out together, and said to him, 'Sir, the Devil is very angry at you, for he thinks you are coming in on his quarters to spoil and rob him of souls; and he is doing all he can to faint and discourage you, by raising all that sculduddery work against you! But be not discouraged, for God is doing much good by your ministry, and the Devil is very angry at you'. And when Mr Glendinning went throu the merkat place, to go away from my father, he cryed out, 'Bless God for your minister'".

In 1658 Glendinning was appointed to Row on the Gareloch, again in a temporary capacity "till a way of planting a minister having the Highland language be obtained". He was still there when the religious persecution in the reign of Charles II began and in 1662, like so many other ministers, he was "outed" from his parish. When John Stirling commented on the sad times through which the Presbyterian Church was passing, his old friend replied cheerfully, "Very good times, very good times indeed, for honest men are now kent to be honest men and knaves to be knaves". In February 1663, Glendinning being "ane old infirm man of the age of fourscore years" petitioned the Privy Council for his stipend for the previous year, which had been confiscated. His request was granted "in respect that his son James had been executed for adherence to the Royalist cause". He seems to have returned to Ireland, where he died.

JOHN WALLACE

If James Glendinning enjoyed a quiet and relatively peaceful ministry, the same can hardly be said of his successor. John Wallace, born about 1629, graduated at the University ofGlasgow in 1649, and married Jane, daughter of the Rev. George Hutchison, minister of Irvine. Wallace was admitted to Largs in 1658 and was to be minister there in troubled times. His resolute stand against Episcopacy added a notable page in the annals of the Parish of Largs. He came of a stock that was morally certain to meet ecclesiastical persecution more than halfway, being a close kinsman of the celebrated James Wallace of Auchans, a colonel in the Foot Guards, who fought for Parliament in the civil wars; was taken prisoner at Kilsyth and again at Dunbar and who led the Covenanting forces at Rullion Green in 1666.

In May 1659, the new minister of Largs and one of his ruling elders, Sir Robert Montgomerie of Skelmorlie, as Glasgow correspondents, attended a meeting at Inverary of the Synod of Argyll. There they raised the matter of "some people in Arran who never hear sermon". The Synod appointed preachers to go to the island on two Sabbaths in June and one in July to instruct the people in the grounds of religion; adding with some severity, "especially the people about Lochransey".

But Wallace's early ministry soon witnessed large-scale participation by his parishioners in less creditable episodes than the spread of the Gospel. In the late 16th century and for much of the

17th, Scotland experienced successive waves of witch hunting. The need to search out and circumvent those in league with the powers of darkness was clear to all right-thinking people. Sincere clergymen and committed congregations saw it as an integral part of their Christian duty and the General Assembly issued repeated instructions to ministers and church courts to be vigilant against the sin of witchcraft. Records show that from time to time Presbyteries and Kirk Sessions could not meet and sometimes even the regular church services had to be abandoned because ministers were absent on the track of witches. And once the hunt was up, neuroses, hallucinations, the craving for notoriety, and sheer spite could combine to produce accusations and confessions to appal the righteous.

The Presbytery of Irvine became engrossed in one of these periodic witch-hunts and Largs was shown to be a centre of fearful activity. Of course, for generations local people had heard of unholy events at "The Back of the World" in the bleak moorland between Largs and Inverkip. But these were tales to frighten bairns or to induce sensations of delicious horror around the fireside on winter evenings. The Presbytery investigations were a very different matter. The minutes of 30th April 1660, noted

> "that some of the brethren did convene to receive and examine the confession of Maal Montgomerie of Largs, Mall Small of Largs and Isobel Maillshead of Largs, who had confessed ilk ane of them of their guiltiness of the sin of witchcraft, and after examination of the aforesaid confessions they are found relevant to be recommended for issuing forth of a commission to put them to assize the seventh May, 1660. Because there is to be ane execution of four persons, three of them being the aforesaid from Largs, upon Saturday next at Irvine for the sin of Witchcraft, the Presbytery does appoint three ministers, viz Mr James Ferguson, Mr Matthew Mowat and Mr Andrew Hutchison, together with the minister of the place, to attend the execution the said day".

Around the same period, the industrious and righteous court seems also to have dealt with five other local women: Sarah Erskine, Jean King, Katie Scott, Janet Holm, and Maria Lamont. The last-named was "burnt". The fate of the others does not seem to have been recorded but few charged with witchcraft were ever acquitted. Even if the death penalty was not exacted there was so much wanton cruelty towards these hapless women that few survived. There is a record of a suspected witch "quha hangit herself in prison". She was probably not the only one. A final round-up of local witches took place in 1662 when the Privy Council gave orders for the trial of six self-confessed witches – Janet Crawford, Jean Dunbar,Agnes Clark, Janet Whyte, Marjorie Scott, and Christian Small – all of them described as "indwellers in Largs". What happened to them is not recorded, perhaps because by this time Presbytery and local congregation had abandoned the excitements of witch baiting for matters of more immediate concern.

Scotland welcomed the Restoration of King Charles II with enthusiasm. There were festive banquets and fireworks as well as solemn services of thanksgiving. The euphoria was short lived. Almost immediately the supreme power in the Church reverted to the monarchy. Episcopacy was re-established; bishops re-appointed and lay patronage restored. The General Assembly fell into abeyance though Presbyteries and Kirk Sessions were permitted to function and there was little interference with forms of worship. The Restoration ecclesiastical settlement was a curious combination of Presbyterianism under Episcopalian government. It was an unsatisfactory compromise, which pleased few and goaded the extreme Covenanting party into a fanaticism that was ultimately to lead them to armed rebellion.

In 1662 Parliament declared that all incumbents inducted into their parishes since 1649 – when patronage had been abolished – must before the 20th September obtain the formal approval of their patrons and apply to their bishops for official appointment to their benefices. Many refused on the grounds that to do so would imply that, lacking these preliminaries, their ministries had been invalid. On 1st October the Privy Council ordered that all who failed to comply must leave their parishes by 1st November. The date was later extended, but to the surprise of the Church authorities, most ministers in the south-west refused to submit. Churches were closed; manses and parishes abandoned; and even the arrears of stipend due for the previous year were relinquished. A historian of the time writes of these ministers,

> "They were not only deprived of their livings in time to come, but also of the year's stipend for which they had served, and, in the winter season, obliged with sorrowful hearts and empty pockets to wander and I know not how many miles with their numerous and small families, many of them scarce knew whither. But the Lord wonderfully provided for them and theirs, to their own confirmation and wonder".

John Wallace of Largs was one of almost 300 "outed" ministers.

PETER TRUMBLE

The Church authorities were acutely embarrassed by the need to fill so many unexpected vacancies. Prompt action had to be taken to re-open the churches and, as a result, standards for admission to the ministry were unavoidably lowered. The men who took the places of the outed ministers were met with scorn and were generally described as "curates", the word being used as a term of contempt. A gentleman in the north, it was said, cursed the Presbyterian ministers because, he said,

> "since they left their churches we cannot get a lad to keep our cows; they all turn ministers".

Even the Episcopalian Bishop Burnet had doubts. He observed:

> "there was a sort of an invitation sent over the kingdom like a hue-and-cry, to all persons to accept of benefices in the west. The livings were generally well endowed, and the parsonage houses were well built and in good repair; and this drew many very worthless persons thither, who had little learning, less piety and no sort of discretion ...They were a disgrace to their orders and the sacred function".

The curates were probably less ignorant and less immoral than their detractors suggested, but, however well meaning they might have been, they were unlikely to win the respect of congregations forced to receive them.

The government gave them what suppport it could. Outed ministers were forbidden to go within twenty miles of their former parishes; private services and open air preachings were declared illegal; and fines were exacted for non-attendance at church. Yet the curates remained on sufferance.

Peter Trumble – the name is the older form of Turnbull – was licensed by the Presbytery of Paisley and was appointed in 1664 to officiate at Largs in the absence of the minister. Nothing more is known about him though he had the care of the congregation for almost ten years. In that time he may have acquired some acceptance but, unless Largs was very different from other places, he would never be regarded as anything other than an interloper usurping the place of the "real" minister.

By 1671 Peter Trumble was no longer in Largs, although the reason for his leaving is not known. The vacant stipend of the parish, along with those from Dundonald, Kilbarchan, and Neilston, was passed to the Earl of Dundonald for the relief of the widow and family of Dr Robert Barron, Professor of Theology at Aberdeen, in view of their great sufferings for his loyalty, and their continued impoverishment. No doubt the Barron children began to thrive again on the fruits of the Largs benefice; though the minister who would not win them back at the price of conscience, continued, outlawed and impecunious, to face further persecution and a yet sterner struggle.

One other event of the year 1671 was of some moment in the parish. The ancient family of Kelso of Kelsoland, dating as far back as the Ragman Roll of 1296, sold their mansion and estate to James Brisbane of Bishoptoun.

JOHN WALLACE

Many of the outed ministers returned secretly to their former parishes from time to time. There is no absolute proof that John Wallace visited Largs but it would have been quite in character for him to have done so, and if he did, there is no doubt that the general dissatisfaction would have ensured him a warm welcome. The government saw all opposition to its religious policies as insurrection and adopted increasingly severe measures to stamp it out. So far as the ordinary people were concerned, fines for non-attendance at church and other petty misdemeanours were summary and unrecorded. The landowners' transgressions were better documented. Robert Kelso of Kelsoland was fined £800 and both James Brisbane of Brisbane and Sir Robert Montgomerie of Skelmorlie were ordered to restrain their wives from attending conventicles. No details are given as to when and where the ladies were present at these open air preachings and there is neither evidence nor tradition of conventicles being held in the Parish of Largs, but in the prevalent discontent there may well have been illegal services in cottages, in the lairds' houses, or out of doors.

An alternative church developed in south-west Scotland and the contrast between it and the worship as established by law can perhaps best be summed up by two quotations. On the one hand there was the old woman who declared gleefully that she had become
> "that deaf, ye ken, I can get nae ill from the Curate's preaching".

On the other hand there were the groups of people who met together echoing the sentiment, if not the actual words, of the Rev. J Welsh of Ayr:
> "We are met this day in the name of our Lord Jesus Christ, the King and Head of His Church. These meetings ye know are forbidden by authority; but there is One greater than they that commands to the contrary of what they command, and His command must be obeyed".

In 1666 unrest flared into armed revolt in the Pentland Rising. It was easy enough for the government forces to overcome about 1,000 badly armed and untrained men, but the draconian measures adopted against the prisoners added fuel to the smouldering fires of bitterness. The authorities were thoroughly alarmed. They suspected – falsely as it happened – that there had been political motives behind the rising and that insurgents might make common cause with the Dutch, who were then at war with England. The government made an attempt to distinguish between nonconformity and sedition. It was decided that evicted ministers who were willing to give undertakings for their future good behaviour might return to their parishes. But the restrictions placed on this First Indulgence were so extreme that few took advantage of it. One who did was the Rev. George Hutchison of Irvine. His son-in-law, John Wallace, did not; and indeed within the year Wallace was again in trouble, being charged, along with a group of uncompromising colleagues, with preaching and baptising irregularly.

The government made a second endeavour at reconciliation, this time accompanied by threats against those who refused to submit. Conditions attached to the Second Indulgence of 1672 were still stringent. Ministers allowed to return to their charges must not travel outwith their parish boundaries unless with special permission; they must all celebrate the Lord's Supper on the same day, to prevent sacramental pilgrimages bringing together great assemblies of the disaffected; they must not baptise or marry persons from parishes other than their own; they must conduct services only in the church and under no circumstances out of doors; they must not, from the pulpit or in the parish, use language that could be construed as an attack on the King; and finally, they must each year loyally celebrate 29th May as the anniversary of the restoration of the monarchy.

After ten years of exile from his parish, John Wallace decided to give this new form of ministry a trial. He returned to his duties in Largs on 3rd September 1672, but he did not return alone. It had been decreed that he must share his pulpit and his stipend with another indulged minister, the Rev. Alexander Gordon.

ALEXANDER GORDON

Alexander Gordon graduated Master of Arts at Glasgow University in 1644. He was subsequently described as "the Marquis of Argyle his chaplain" and was admitted minister of Inveraray. Ousted from that parish by the enactments of 1662, he suffered "great hardship and sore persecution" and was ill for some time of "a very dangerous fever and near to death". However, he survived and in 1668 was an "indweller at Kilmory". In 1672 he was indulged along with John Wallace to preach at Largs and seems to have officiated also at Greenock.

He gave further offence by keeping a conventicle in Glasgow. The magistrates there were ordered in June 1676 to produce him and, having failed to do so for three years, were subjected to a fine in 1679. It is not clear for how many years Gordon remained as Wallace's colleague in Largs, but by 1688 he was minister of the parish of Greenock. Under the Toleration introduced in the reign of

King James VII, Gordon returned to Inveraray and carried on his ministry there until illness and old age forced him to demit office about the turn of the century. He retired to Glasgow where he died on 20th March 1713, being then about 89 years of age and "Father of the Church" in Scotland. He is credited with having "a singular talent for lecturing" and published an account of the General Assembly held at St Andrews in 1651, having outlived all other members of that Assembly.

The Rev. Alexander Gordon appears as minister of Inveraray in Neil Munro's novel *John Splendid*.[17]

JOHN WALLACE

When John Wallace returned to Largs in 1672, the parish must have been in a state of some unrest. In that year the government issued a decree that 500 Scots seamen should be impressed for service against the threats of the Dutch navy, with powers for their apprehension and under pain of a heavy fine. Largs was to provide three men; Fairlie two; and Kelburn one. Unfortunately the names of these conscripts have not survived. In ecclesiastical matters, official attempts at reconciliation were reinforced by more extreme punishments for those who continued to resist. Conventicles and field communions were on the increase, and in an effort to suppress them, heritors and masters were made responsible for the good behaviour of their tenants and servants. They had to undertake that neither they nor any of their dependents would attend conventicles, harbour or have any other dealings with the peripatetic preachers, and that they would hand over to the law all who disregarded the State's religious legislation. In 1677 an Act brought into force an almost complete boycott of dissenters; and in the following year, landowners and masters were required to sign bonds on behalf of all persons, whomsoever, residing in their lands. Not unnaturally, many refused to undertake obligations that it would have been quite impossible to fulfil and the government, in a final endeavour at

intimidation, ordered the "Highland Host" – a body of some 3,000 Lowland militia and 6,000 Highlanders – into the south-west. They swept through Ayrshire, forcing landowners to sign the Bond, punishing those who refused and disarming the country. As church and churchyard were the recognised rallying points of any country community, a Glasgow decree of 29th January 1678 called upon
> "the Largs heretours, lyferenters, conjunct fiars, tenants,cotters and others to disarm on 13th February at the Kirk of Largs".

However many weapons were handed over at Largs, it became clear in the following year that in other places a fair proportion had been secreted away for future use.

It was hardly to be expected that John Wallace would be disposed to abide by the stated terms of his Indulgence as a docile minister. His strong Presbyterian principles soon had him involved in fresh trouble. On 14th July 1674, a warrant was issued for his apprehension on a renewed charge of conventicle preaching. He seems to have evaded punishment on this occasion, but by 7th November 1678, another complaint was made to the Privy Council. It stated that the minister of Largs had several times preached in other pulpits and had kept conventicles in Renfrewshire and Ayrshire. Also he
> "hath had the boldness and impudence to refuse and deny the benefite of the sacrament of baptisme to the children of some persons within the said paroch of Larges because their parents, in obedience to his Majesties commands, had subscrived the band for the publicke peace of the Kingdome".

Upon Wallace refusing to bind himself to baptise the children of those who bowed to State dictation, the Privy Council
> "decern the said Mr John Wallace to have lost the benefit of the indulgence and discharge him to preach at Larges or any place else ... and appoints this their sentence to be intimated to the pariochiners to the end they may not heir him nor pay stipend to him for the future".

So in 1679, John Wallace was once again deprived and driven from the parish of Largs.

CHARLES LITTLEJOHN

John Wallace left Largs in February of 1679. That year, as it progressed, brought events of greater significance in Scottish history.

In May a group of extremist Covenanters accidentally met Archbishop Sharp near St Andrews and killed him. The murderers fled to the south-west where they gathered a band of supporters. On 1st June a body of dragoons attempted to break up a conventicle at which many of the worshippers were armed. The military were driven off in what the Covenanters regarded as the glorious victory of the Battle of Drumclog. But by the end of the month, government forces had decisively crushed the rebellion at Bothwell Brig.

The inevitable reprisals followed, though indemnity was granted to those who undertook never again to take up arms against the King nor to frequent field conventicles. Dragoons scoured the countryside in search of malignants and any who refused to give the required pledges were executed as rebels, often without trial. The years after 1679 came to be known as "The Killing Time". It must be remembered that only a minute proportion of the population actively engaged in revolt; that executions were fewer than is sometimes supposed; and that those who were killed had, as self-confessed rebels and troublemakers, given the government every encouragement to proceed against them. Yet the great majority of the ordinary people of the south-west were in wholehearted sympathy with the cause of the Covenanters and many had a sincere piety and a fervent devotion to their idealised vision of Christ's Kirk on earth. Then, and later, they drew their heroes and martyrs from the ranks of the Covenanters.

Discontent extended also into the field of civil legislation. As a result of the disturbances in Ireland, the import of goods and cattle from that country was severely restricted. The decree, which specifically named Largs among the seaboard parishes affected, laid down that

> "skippers or owners of boates, barkes or other vessells travelling to and frae the places foresaids are hereby ordered before they break bulk or liver any goodes to advertise the saids commissioners ... under pain of confiscation".

The Privy Council Register for 1679 records that William Steven of Largs having brought in from Ireland "severall bags of meall" was imprisoned by order of the Earl of Dundonald. His meal was "staved" and his boat burned. Nor was it always a distant nobleman like Dundonald who exacted the penalty. In 1679 and again in 1680, John Boyle of Kelburn was granted powers to enforce these laws over a wide stretch of water from Loch Long to Galloway, including Bute, Arran, and the Cumbraes. In 1681 a Test Act, designed to suppress the last vestiges of the Covenants, required all who held public office of any kind to renounce the Covenants; acknowledge the King's supremacy in both church and state; avoid conventicles; and never again rise in arms against the government. Commissioners, whose chief duty was to enforce this law, inclued John Boyle.

Brief minutes in official documents prove that at this time Largs was not a complete backwater. The Earl of Dumbarton, who was "General Leivetenent of His Majesties Forces", issued an order:
> "Upon sight of this, see that the bearer Archibald Shearer's horse be delivered to him, he going to the Largs for the King's service. Given at Glasgow this 10 day of June, 1685 (Signed) Dumbarton".

A further note added:
> "Send a boat with him aboard one of the King's men of war lyeing nearest".

The Privy Council in July of the same year instructed Dumbarton
> "to search for the arms and ammunition stored by the late Earl of Argyle and his rebels in the tounes of Greenock, Larges, Irving and Gourock".

Four years later freight was paid for twelve boats to transport soldiers from Largs to Kintyre and on another occasion the people of Largs were commanded to "furnish and provide magizones of hay, corne and straw" sufficient to supply "one hundred horses at Largs for the space of eight days". Troops on their way to troubled Ireland were to be "furnished with the provissiones abovementioned ... at eassie and reasonable rates for the said corne, hay and straw".

It was against this background that Charles Littlejohn served as the last of the Episcopalian curates in Largs. He was a graduate of St Andrews University and had been Regent of Humanity at St Salvator's College there. On 19th July 1684, he married Mary Ramsay and, in later years, their son George was Snell Exhibitioner at Oxford. Charles Littlejohn was ordained and admitted as minister of Largs on 26th May, 1680. His tenure of office was to continue until the troubles of the Presbyterian Church were virtually over. And, curiously enough, more is known about Largs Church under Charles Littlejohn than under any of his predecessors.

The parish ministers of Ayrshire were summoned to Ayr to report on the state of their churches and the behaviour of their parishioners and, fortunately, the detailed report on the Kirk of Largs given on 21st and 22nd October 1684, survives in the Register of the Privy Council:

"Mr Charles Littlejohn, minister at Largs, being solemnlie sworne and interogat, depons that the list of his parochers, heritors and elders given in and signed by him is a full and true list according to the deponents knowledge; depons that he hes bein minister at Largs these four years bygone, in which tyme he hes not given the sacrament of the Lords Supper, having bein hindered therfrom at his first comeing to the paroch by his parochers iregularities and having bein bussied ever since in instructing and examining them to fitt them therfor, and the greatest part of the men of his paroch bein imployed in seafareing; depons that he is verie well pleased with his session, they being verie ordorlie and assistant to him, and that ther are non nowe within his paroch to the deponents knowledge who doe not come to church; depons ther is no chaplands in his paroch; depones he knowes of no rebells nor recepters of them within his paroch, nor the wives or widdowes of any, excepting Margaret Barcley, relict of William Rosse, a vagrant chapman, whom wes said to [have] bein at the rebellion, depons she is regular; depons he knowes of no chapmen in his paroch; depons that hears ther is on Robert Forrest in Fairlie and James Thomson in Gogosyd, who have either baptized ther children irregularlie or keept them up from baptizme a considerable tyme, and this is all he knowes and the truth, as he shall answer to God (Signed) Charles Littlejohn.

Air 22 October, 1684.The quhilk day, in presence of Pattrick Ramsay, colector in Air, apointed be the Lords of the Comitie of his Majesties Privie Counsell for taking the oathes and depositiones of the persones afternamit, elders and deacones within the parish of Larges, upon the interogators afterspecifeit. In the first compeired Robert Harvie in Larges, whoe being present, upon oath, of the age of 50 yeirs or therby, maried, depones he knowes none within the said parish of Larges whoe frequents not the ordinances; depones he knowes of noe conventicles or other disorderlie meitings within the said parish; depones he knowes of noe rebells or fugatives wyves therin except the relict of ane William Rosse, ane rebell, whoe died in Kintyre, and that shoe dailie frequents the ordinances; depones he shall be assistant to the minister in giving up the list of the parishoners; depones he knowes of none gone furth of the said parish except ane Alexander Boyd, whoe is removit to the parish of Killbryd, where ther is ane indulged minister and that to the best of his knoueledge is the cause of his removing, and that ane David Wallace is also removed to the best of his knowledge for the same cause; depones he knoues of noe packmen within the said parish, except ane James Jamiesone under the Craige; depones he knowes none oficiating in any publict trust not taking the Test; depones he knowes none fitter in the paroch to give up ane acompt therof then himself and the rest of the elders; all quhich is the treuth, as he shall answer to God, and addes he knowes of none that hes baptized their childrein irregularlie and knowes of noe chaplaines within the said parish. (Signed) Robert Hervie.

James Craufurd in Skellmurlie, present, upon oath, of the age of 48 yeires or therby, maried, depones idem, which is the treuth, as he shall ansuer to God, and cannot wryt.

James Craig in Skellmurlie, present, upon oath, of the age of 60 yeirs or therby, maried, depones idem, quhich is the treuth, as he shall ansuer to God, and cannot wryt

John Craufurd in Thridpart, of the age of 50 yeirs or therby, maried, depones idem, which [is] the treuth, as he shall ansuer to God (Signed) John Craufurd.

John Small in Dyckes, present upon oath, of the age of 55 yeirs or therby, maried, depones idem, quhich is the treuth, as he shall ansuer to God, and cannot wryt.

Hew Craufurd in Knock, present, upon oath, of the age of 56 yeirs or therby, maried, depones idem, which is the treuth, as he shall ansuer to God and cannot wryt.

John Finnie in Grassyeards, present upon oath, of the age of 60 yeirs or therby, maried, depones idem, quhich is the treuth, as he shall ansuer to God, and cannot wryt.

Robert Morreis in Bankheide, present, upon oath, of the age of 40 years or therby, maried, depones idem with the former, and addes one Robert Kyll, ane packman, which is the treuth, as he shall ansuer to God, and cannot wryt.

Hendry Niniane in Kirkland, present, upon oath, of the age of 68 yeirs or therby, maried, depones idem, quhich is the treuth, etc, and cannot wryt.

Hew Pattoune in Constablewood, present, upon oath, of the age of 50 yeirs or therby, maried, depones idem, quhich is the treuth, as he shall answer to God, and cannot wryt.

John Broune in Tourgill, present, upon oath, of the age of 36 yeirs or therby, maried, depones idem, which is the treuth, as he shall ansuer to God, and cannot wryt.

William Andrew in Tourgill, present, upon oath, of the age of 65 yeirs or thereby, maried, depones idem, and cannot wryt.

James Craufurd in Whittlieburne, upon oath, of the age of 60 yeirs, unmaried, depones idem, which is the treuth, as he shall ansuer to God, and cannot wryt.

John Beith ther, present, upon oath, of the age of 40 yeirs or therby, maried, depones idem, quhich is the treuth, as he shall ansuer to God. (Signed) J Beith.

Alexander Boyd in Noddsdaill, present, upon oath, of the age of 70 yeirs, maried, depones idem, which is the treuth, as he shall ansuer to God, and cannot wryt.

Thomas Jamiesone in Douchray, upon oath, of the age of 50 yeirs or therby, maried, depones idem. (Signed) Thomas Jamisoune.

Robert Bartle in Larges, present, upon oath, of the age of 30 yeirs or therby, maried, depones idem, quhich is the treuth, as he shall ansuer to God. (Signed) Robert Bartley.

Cornellius Thomsone in Gogerside, present, upon oath, of the age of 50 yeirs or theirby, maried, depones idem with the former, and addes that their is ane, James Thomsone in Boghouseside, that hes ane child irregularlie baptized and, as he is informed, was baptized be Mr Alexander Simers, lait minister at Cumrays, quhich is the treuth, as he shall ansuer to God, and cannot wryt.

John Willsone of Hallie, present, upon oath, of the age of 40 yeirs or therby, maried, depones idem, quhich is the treuth, as he shall ansuer to God, and cannot wryt.

John Wyllie in Watterside, present, upon oath, of the age of 50 yeirs or therby, married, depones idem with the former, and addes that Robert Foster in Fairlie has ane child not baptised with the minister, quich is the treuth, as he shall ansuer to God, and cannot wryt."

It is of some interest that the Scottish Church had for more than a century paid lip-service to education but that out of the twenty office-bearers who testified, only five had attained the very moderate literacy required to sign their own names.

For a brief moment the Kirk of Largs can be clearly seen. One may suspect that the imperative seafaring duties of the men were perhaps excuses rather than reasons for their absence from church, but one can picture Charles Littlejohn conscientiously striving to lead his parishioners to a suitable frame of mind in which to receive the Eucharist. Admittedly there were defaulters, but they are mentioned with a singular lack of acrimony; and if there is not a great deal of enthusiasm in the report it does at least show that, whatever undercurrents there may have been, the work of the church was being faithfully carried out in spite of difficulties.

Meantime, in the country as a whole events were careering towards a climax. In 1685 Charles II died and was succeeded by his brother James, who almost immediately instituted a policy of religious toleration. Though this was obviously intended to give freedom of worship to the new king's fellow Roman Catholics, and as such was hardly calculated to appeal to his Scottish subjects, "The Toleration" had to include other denominations and the Presbyterians benefited.

Ousted ministers were allowed to return to their parishes. Services out of doors were forbidden – the authorities were still terrified of what they saw only as potential hotbeds of sedition – but ministers could conduct Presbyterian services for those who wished to attend in private houses or other suitable buildings.

The Presbyterian Church began to organise itself as a nonconformist body by setting up their own Presbyteries alongside, but distinct from, those of the Episcopalian establishment. John Wallace returned to Largs and was present at the first meeting of the reconstituted Presbytery of Irvine on 17th August, 1687. He may perhaps have found his position distasteful as a dissenting clergyman conducting hole and corner services while the Episcopalian Littlejohn occupied the church and drew the stipend. Whether or not that was his reason, Wallace left Largs late in 1687 or early in 1688, and retired to his estate at Monkcastle near Kilwinning. After the re-establishment of the Presbyterian Church he was inducted as minister to the Border parish of Mertoun on 13th May 1692, and died there the following year.

King James VII embroiled himself with his English subjects, some of whom invited his elder daughter Mary, and her Protestant husband Prince William of Orange, to accept the English crown. Scotland hesitated – long enough for James Montgomerie of Thirdpart and Blackhouse to be forfeited for having commanded a company in the forces that supported the Dutch invasion – but by the end of 1688 William and Mary had been accepted as King and Queen in Scotland and James VII had fled into exile on the Continent.

Once the downfall of James VII was assured, the ordinary people of south-west Scotland took the law into their own hands. In a

spontaneous popular outburst, they drove the Episcopalian clergymen out of their manses and parishes in December, 1688. There was no bloodshed but little consideration for families turned out of their homes in mid-winter. How Charles Littlejohn was evicted from Largs is not known but in his flight he met up with the curate from West Kilbride, who had been "rabbled" out of that parish in quite spectacular fashion, having been
> "buffetted and stoned by an angry crowd from the manse, down by Coldstream and Nethermilne to the south".

The two unfortunate clergymen joined forces and were together in hiding for some time, "separated from their families, their whereabouts unknown". Charles Littlejohn did not return to Largs. He was deprived on 25th April 1690, by the Act of Parliament restoring the Presbyterian ministers, and died in Edinburgh on 12th November 1732, at the age of 82.

A new constitution for the Scottish Church was worked out and ratified by William II in 1690. It was to remain in force until the 20th century. Presbyterianism with its hierarchy of courts: General Assembly, synods, presbyteries and kirk sessions, was established with its theology and worship based on the Westminster Confession of Faith, and lay patronage was again abolished. It was the only lawful Church in Scotland and the vast majority of Scots were either committed to it or gave it nominal adherence. Two groups remained outside it. In the south-west, the Cameronians regarded it as a compromise with the state which was not compatible with the Covenants. They formed the Reformed Presbyterian Church which continued outwith the mainstream of Scottish Presbyterianism, though it did not engage in political activity. In 1876 the majority of its members united with the Free Church of Scotland and today only a tiny remnant survives. At the other extreme, those who were committed to Episcopalian doctrines and forms of worship and those who, believing that James VII was their true King, were unwilling to give allegiance to his successors or even to engage in public prayers for them, formed the Scottish Episcopal Church. Its main strength was in the north-east but small groups developed sporadically elsewhere in the country. Loyalty to the House of

Stuart involved the Scottish Episcopalians in the Jacobite Risings of 1715 and 1745; but for that, the motives were purely political. The Scottish wars of religion were finally over.

JOHN WILSON

The Settlement of 1690 established the Presbyterian Church in Scotland but did not solve its problems. The long Episcopalian domination had resulted in a dearth of qualified ministers and for many years "the great business of the General Assembly was placing vacant parishes", and occasionally supplying them with itinerant preachers until they were "planted". John Wallace left Largs probably late in 1687 and Charles Littlejohn was ejected in December, 1688. On 22nd January 1689, John Wilson was admitted minister of Largs.

Born in Ayrshire in 1653, John Wilson graduated Master of Arts at the University of Edinburgh in 1678. There is no evidence as to how he was employed until he was ordained in 1684 as minister of Dunboe in Ulster. Like many other Presbyterian ministers, he fled from the disturbed political situation in Ireland in 1689. He returned to Ayrshire, and after declining a call to Kilmarnock was settled temporarily at Largs. By 1691 the Synod of Ulster was anxious that those ministers who had left the country "contrary to their express obligations to their respective charges and to the Church of Ireland" should return to their duties. The Presbytery of Irvine wrote to the Synod requesting that Wilson be freed from his charge in Dunboe, but as none of the parties concerned was present, the Synod refused to take any action regarding the transfer. Despite this, Wilson was soon afterwards permanently settled in Largs, although the Ulster Synod continued for some years to write both to the Presbytery and Wilson himself about his recall to what it still regarded as his official charge.

Nothing is known about John Wilson's ministry in Largs but some traces have survived of his work elsewhere in the district. In June 1691, he was one of several ministers who assisted at Communion services in Kilwinning, and this introduces what was to become in country parishes a feature of Church life in the 18th century.

At this time the observance of the Lord's Supper was a most solemn occasion but it was held much less frequently than it is today. Sometimes a parish would have no Communion of its own for several years: indeed, one minister served the parish of Carsphairn for sixteen years without a single celebration. Consequently, when it became known that the Sacrament was to be dispensed at, say, Dalry, the parishioners of Beith, Dunlop, Stewarton, and Kilmaurs would flock there from the east; those of Ardrossan, Kilbride, and Largs would cross the hills from the west; people would arrive from Kilwinning, Stevenson, Irvine, and Dreghorn in the south and others from the northerly parishes of Kilbirnie, Lochwinnoch, and even Paisley. Indeed, wherever what came to be referred as "The Occasion" was celebrated, there would be a great gathering of people. And not only for services on the Sabbath.

The religious observances might well start on Thursday so that those who wished to attend would quarter themselves on the local population, straining the limits of hospitality to the extreme. Most houses in the township would have their quota of guests and at the farms there could be possibly fifty or a hundred guests – in one case the number of 180 is quoted – sleeping in makeshift beds with the women preparing an endless supply of meals. Work in the district would be suspended for the long weekend, and it was not unusual for servants and labourers, as a condition of their terms of employment, to be given time off to attend one Occasion annually. Such a gathering provided more than religious activity. There were opportunities for social contacts, business deals, and courting. Alehouses would do good business and young men and women, dressed in their best, would parade the streets. Hawkers, travelling tinkers, packmen, and beggars would be attracted by the crowds. In fact, the Occasion was almost identical with the annual fairs held in market towns except that it was overlaid with religious duties and that, for some at least, spiritual matters would take precedence. Robert Burns in his poem The Holy Fair sums up the curious mixture of the sacred and the profane.

In the adjoining parishes many church records would show the entry "No sermon this Lord's Day", for the ministers, like many of their parishioners, would have gone to assist at the Occasion.

Not all of the intending communicants would arrive on the Thursday which was a Fast Day. It is not certain whether there was ever any abstinence from food but the day was observed like a Sunday: only essential work was done; recreation was not permitted; and religious exercises began with tent preachings. The so-called "tent" was, in fact, a small wooden erection not unlike a sentry box set up in the churchyard or on some other suitable open space where crowds could assemble in front of it. Its mission was to give shelter from wind and rain to the succession of ministers who would occupy it during the weekend, but it also served as a sounding box which enabled preachers to address and be heard by quite an extensive gathering of listeners. Although Friday reverted to being rather an ordinary day, the tent preachings continued and on Saturday they became increasingly solemn as preparations were made for "the Great Wark" – the actual observance of the Sacrament. This took place within the church but, as it could not possibly accommodate so many people, services began early on Sunday morning and were conducted throughout the day by relays of ministers. Preachings from the tent continued for those who had already received Communion or were awaiting admission. Monday would begin with services of thanksgiving and finally one of the ministers would, from the tent, "close the work" by summarising the addresses given by his colleagues during the weekend and by delivering some uplifting thought for his hearers to bear in mind until the next Occasion. Thereafter the clergymen would retire, no doubt exhausted, to the Manse and their parishioners would be free to enjoy themselves for the rest of the day. In the evening they would set out to trudge the many miles back to their homes and their everyday lives as described by Burns:

"There's some are fou o' love divine;
There's some are fou o' brandy;"

The more popular the preachers chosen to assist the local minister, the larger the influx of visitors and the greater the drain on local resources. In spite of the spiritual uplift, the social enjoyment and, not least, the large collections uplifted for the Poor Fund, it can cause little surprise that once the Holy Fair was ended local people were quite well pleased to forego another celebration for several years.

The loss of the Largs Kirk Session records means that there is no remaining picture of an old Largs Communion at this period. Whether John Wilson, or his successors, erected a preaching tent beside the Skelmorlie Aisle or on the Green, or whether the local Occasion ever attained the excessive numbers recorded at Holy Fairs elsewhere must remain unknown. No tradition has survived and it may well be that Largs celebrated the Sacrament more modestly; but even so, local people would know of, and perhaps some would travel to, Communions held in neighbouring parishes and from time to time the minister would be called upon to assist at them.

During John Wilson's ministry a quite significant contribution was made in the field of education. The Presbytery of Ardrossan in 1696, when Wilson was its Moderator, reported to Parliament on the state of schools in ten parishes. At the head of this assessment came Irvine, which stood alone in having a schoolmaster provided with a salary, a school, and a dwelling house. In the next category, Largs along with Kilbirnie and Fenwick had each a schoolmaster with a salary, but had made no arrangements for premises. Dunlop apparently did not have a parochial schoolmaster, but an independent teacher held classes in a school with house attached which had been built and endowed by the titled son of a former minister.

In Ardrossan, Beith, and Kilbirnie premises were lacking and although there was a salary, the posts of schoolmaster in these parishes were vacant at the time of the report. Finally, Kilmaurs and Dreghorn were both reported to have made no provision whatsoever for education. It seems odd that Kilwinning was not included in the report. Certainly there was a schoolmaster, for William Smith taught there before becoming minister in Largs and in the same year as the report, the Largs parochial schoolmaster, John Maclean, transferred his services and his tawse to Kilwinning.

Education had from the beginning been in the forefront of the programme of the Reformed Church in Scotland although enactments

on the subject were often ignored. However, in spite of the disturbed political and religious situation, considerable progress had been made during the 17th century. In 1696 an Act of Parliament ordained
> "that there be a Schoole founded and a Schoolmaster appointed in every parish not already provided, by advice of the Presbyteries; and to this purpose that the heritors in every congregation meet among themselves and provide a commodious house for a Schoole and modify a stipend for a Schoolmaster, which shall not be under ane hundred merks nor above twa hundred merks to be paid yearly at two terms".

The General Assembly followed up this measure with injunctions to the Presbyteries and, although it was quite a long time before the Act was fully implemented, it did inaugurate the Scottish Parish School system. The church appointed schoolmasters, conducted examinations in religious knowledge, and imposed doctrinal standards on the teachers. Education was not free – to have made it so, it was thought, would have been to undervalue it – but it was cheap and in most parishes there was the opportunity for the lad of parts to receive a schooling that could set him on his way to future success whatever may have been his social position. Boys and girls of all classes were pupils together and in some parishes it was the tradition that even the laird's son would receive his earliest formal instruction in the parish school.

It can be seen from the report of 1696 that the young people of Largs had rather better educational opportunities than those available in most of the neighbouring parishes. As a result of the State's insistence, the position was even further improved shortly after the Act of 1696 by the building of a school; though the Largs schoolmaster was not to have a house provided for him for more than a century.

The Largs salary was at the lower end of the scale: 100 merks per year – the equivalent of about £5.50 pence. This was not quite so meagre a sum as it sounds today and the schoolmaster would be able to augment it by modest fees from his pupils and by charging small sums for the services that an educated man could provide in the community.

The closing years of the 17th century were a period of some privation in Scotland. The country had been impoverished by war and a series of poor harvests added to the distress. To many it seemed that overseas trade was the only way to improve the economic position and it is not surprising that the dazzling prospectus of the Darien Company lured so many to invest in it. The grandiose project to establish trading posts on each side of the Darien Isthmus linking the commerce of Atlantic and Pacific and occupying a strategic position on the world's trade routes appeared to promise prosperity for the country and untold riches for the shareholders.

An imposing fleet set sail from Leith in July 1698, with some 2,000 would-be colonists, among whom were ten Presbyterian ministers. The latter were to attend to the spiritual needs of both the emigrants and the Darien natives. They were designated in a pastoral letter from the General Assembly "missionary ministers", and in a sense they may be reckoned the pioneers of all the subsequent missionary enterprise of the Church of Scotland.

The scheme failed disastrously. Very few of the colonists survived to return home and many of the shareholders were totally ruined.

It was estimated that Scotland lost almost a third of its resources. Ayrshire alone had subscribed something like £20,000 but it may be some solace to know that in the wild rush of speculation, the stolid parishioners of Largs had adopted a canny attitude. Only three local names appear on the list of Darien shareholders: John Alexander of Blackhouse had invested £200, while Mrs Elizabeth Brisbane and John Kyle, merchant in Largs, had each made the minimum subscription of £100 – though even that was a considerable sum of money then.

But the people of Largs had a more immediate grievance. A measure had been passed granting to the small burghs certain trading privileges that had formerly been limited to the royal burghs in return for the payment of a tax. Specially appointed commissioners, of whom Lord Boyle of Kelburn was one, considered most carefully the matter of the tax to be paid by each burgh. The share for Largs was assessed at £227:18s. Naturally, there was an immediate outcry that the figure was unreasonably high, though the outcome of the protest does not appear to have been preserved.

A few of the Largs people of this time have left their names on the historical record. Sir James Montgomerie of Skelmorlie was one of the Baron Commissioners to Parliament, but as early as 1693 he was fined £600 Scots and deprived of the office for non-attendance. A charter of the period mentions John Crawford of Whitlyburn, William Patton and Elspeth Boys in Kilburn, and William Jamie in Stanely, off Under-Dockray – a placename which survived into the present century in Stanely Cottage beyond Prospecthill.

John Wilson's ministry was comparatively short. He died, aged 46 and unmarried, on 15th November 1699.

ANDREW CUMIN

The new century brought a new minister. He was Andrew Cumin, destined to become the longest serving minister in Largs. He outlived two "assistants and successors" appointed to help him in his old age, and passed his diamond jubilee in the charge by almost a year. His third assistant, Gilbert Lang, did actually succeed him and was minister of Largs until his own death in 1791. The parish was therefore served by only two ministers throughout virtually the whole of the 18th century and this was to have some bearing on its history.

After graduating at Marischal College in Aberdeen, Andrew Cumin became classics master at the school in Irvine. He also acted in some capacity as tutor to the Boyle children, and this no doubt brought him to the notice of Largs. Although lay patronage had been abolished by the Settlement of 1690, selection of a new minister fell not to the congregation in general but to the heritors and elders. Once their choice had been made there was an opportunity for the congregation to approve or disapprove of their nominee and the final decision lay with the Presbytery. The papers concerning Cumin's appointment to Largs survive [18] and the call to Andrew Cumin from the heritors and elders showed no lack of cordiality:

"Undersubscribers, heritors and elders of the Paroch of Largs; considering the great loss that we of this congregation sustean by our continued vacancy, together with the unspeakable gain that may be reaped by the faithful administration of gospel ordinances; and having had occasion at divers times to hear you Mr Andrew Cumine preach the Gospel to our satisfaction and comfort; and been witness of your christian and exemplary conversation of the Doctrine of God our Saviour. Therefore we for ourselves, and in the name of those we represent, doe hereby invit and call you to take the pastoral charge of the inhabitants of this paroch of Largs, when orderly ordeaned and set apart thereunto by the Presbiterie of Irvine; and do obleist you in the bowels of Jesus Christ, that compassioned high priest, to harken to and accept of this our most cordial call; and we earnestly pray that God would incline your heart to comply with this our sincer and unfeigned desire and invition and send you amongst us in the fulness of the blessing of the Gospel, so we do promise our respect and encouragement to you for strengthening your hands in the said work in this place. In testimony we have subscribed their presents at Largs this thirty day of January, ane thousand seven hundred and one years".

It was signed by five heritors and ten elders – among the latter were the names of John Kyd, Robert Barclay, Robert Morise, Wm Beith, Cornelius Thomson, John Crawford, John Jamieson and R Beith – and it was attested by the ministers of Kilbirnie and Kilbride, John Glasgow and George Rennie respectively.

The call was accompanied by a People's Ratification in much the same terms:

" Undersubscribers, inhabitants and heads of families, in the Paroch of Largs, understanding that our herietours and elders have given a call to you Mr Andrew Cumine, preacher of the Gospel, to be our Pastor in dispensing the ministries of Grace and Salvation to us; doe hereby Declair that we are now fully satisfied and content with this their procedor, by giving our hearty consents thereto; but also cordially join with them to entreat and obleist you to embrace the samen; and for our pairts doe promise all obedience, and encouragement to you that a Christian people owes to a faithful Gospel Minister. In witness whereof we have subscribed their presents at Largs, this thirty day of January, ane thousand seven hundred and ane years".

It carried some sixty signatures or attested marks.

Three months later the Presbytery of Ardrossan gave Cumine a testimonial:

"These testify to all whom it may concern that the bearer hereof Mr Andrew Cumin came into ye bounds of ye Presbyterie of Irvine so soon as he had passed his course in Phylosophy in the Colledge of Aberdeen called Marshall's Colledge in the year one thousand six hundred ninety and five, & did abundantly satisfy us as to his carriage and deportment while there by sufficient testimonials thereof. And sine yt time to ye date of thir prest he hath lived amongst us, during which time he hath been imployed partly in teaching ye School of Irvine, partly in being Governour to my Lord Boyle's Children, in both which offices he hath acquitted himself, so far as men can judge, very faithfully, prudently and Christianly to the great satisfaction of all concerned & a good space of that time he hath also officiated as Clerk to ye Prybrie to their very great satisfaction, & in his whole carriage and conversation he hath been so circumspect, blameless and inoffensive yt now at his departure from us we cannot refuse to give him our testimonial and recommend him to the tender care and encouragement of all Minrs & Presbyterys among whom his lot shall fall to be. Given and subscribed at the meeting of the Presbyterie at Irvine the 29 of Aprile ye year one thousand seven hundred and one."

This testimonial was signed by Alex Cunningham, Minister of Dreghorn, the Moderator, and by the ten ministers present at the meeting.

The preliminaries having been duly carried out, Lord Boyle informed the Presbytery in writing that the heritors had agreed that "Mr Cuming" should be admitted to Largs "immediately after Michaelmas Next" and he was ordained and inducted on 27th September, 1701.

Andrew Cumin was unmarried when he arrived in Largs. On 13th July 1703, he married Jean, daughter of John Caldwell of that Ilk, and it would be quite an event in the history of the church when the young minister brought a bride to the Manse. The Cumins had two children: Margaret, who on 10th June 1733, married Hugh Hamilton, merchant in Edinburgh; and John, born in 1714, who also became a minister and was for a brief period his father's colleague.

In the early years of the 18th century the question of the succession to the throne became predominant. James Francis Edward Stuart, in later history to be known as the Old Pretender, was the son of the second marriage of the deposed King James II. He had grown up in exile on the Continent and on his father's death in 1701 he regarded himself as the rightful King of Great Britain and was acknowledged as such by the King of France, with whom England was soon to be at war. Alarmed by the possibility of foreign invasion on behalf of James Stuart's claim, the British Government took steps for the country's defence. According to the Memoirs of John Ker of Kersland in Dalry

"the whole Nation was not only impowered but ordered to Rendezvous and discipline themselves under their own proper Officers as they themselves should chuse. Whereupon they armed immediately, and rendezvoused at every Parish-Church in the Kingdom twice a week; which soon brought the whole Nation to such Perfection in Discipline that they could exercise by Beat of Drum, and perform their other Parts as well as the regular Troops".

Very likely, similar manoeuvres were carried out at Largs, though it must be doubted whether any of the units of this Home Guard ever attained the degree of military efficiency that Ker suggests.

King William II died in 1702 and was succeeded by Anne, the younger daughter of James II. It was already obvious that she would die without a direct heir, and by an Act of Settlement the English Parliament provided that the Crown should pass to her nearest Protestant relative, the Electress Sophia of Hanover and her descendants. This measure did not, of course, apply to Scotland. The Scottish Parliament was free to make its own choice of a future monarch, and might even decide upon the Catholic James Stuart. It seemed that the only practical solution to this, and other problems in the relationship between England and Scotland, was the complete union of the two kingdoms. Negotiations to this end began and among those strongly in favour of union was David Boyle of Kelburn. He had become Lord Boyle in 1699 and in 1702 he was created first Earl of Glasgow. The titles were at once a reward for his services in promoting the idea of union and an incentive to his further efforts. On the other hand, John Brisbane of Brisbane, a Commissioner for Ayrshire in the Scottish Parliament, was equally forceful in resistance to the projected union. With the two leading landowners in direct opposition to each other, the lesser people in the district would probably have equally decided, though less influential, views on the matter. The Union was effected in 1707; it had perhaps become inevitable but it was never to be popular with the ordinary folk.

The Stuarts made their bids for the crown in 1708, 1715, 1719, and 1745. The first Earl of Glasgow supported the Hanoverian cause in 1715 and Thomas Brisbane of Brisbane fought in the government forces at Culloden. Apart from that, Largs seems to have played little active part in the Jacobite Risings. There was, after all, a more profitable and rather less dangerous method of baiting an unpopular government.

The Union Parliament had imposed, and enforced, stringent laws against smuggling. Evading them was not only a useful means of increasing income; it could even be regarded as a patriotic duty. The headland at Portencross was a known resort of smugglers. There, for several years, a certain gentleman – coyly named in official reports reports as "Mr B" – proved a thorn in the flesh of the preventive men. In the Parish of Largs itself there are frequent references to the surreptitious arrival of brandy, rum, tobacco, silk, lace, and playing cards. Handling them could be a welcome addition to more legitimate earnings; but one item of contraband met with some local hostility. Ale was, and had been for generations, the accompaniment of the morning meal. To the orthodox it was unthinkable that it should be superseded by a new-fangled, foreign, and pernicious beverage, and in various parts of the country, people entered into solemn undertakings to abstain from it. So strong was local feeling that in 1740 the "Brisbane Bond", quoted in Graham's *Social Life in Scotland in the Eighteenth Century,* was issued;

> "We bein all farmers by profession, think it needless to restrain ourselves formally from indulging in the foreign and consumptive luxury called tea; for when we consider the slender constitution of many of the higher rank, amongst whom it is most used, we conclude that it would be an improper diet to qualify us for the more robust and manly parts of our business, and therefore only give our testimony against it and leave the enjoyment of it altogether to those who can afford to be weak, indolent, and useless"

Smuggling may have brought a few luxuries to the people of Largs but it probably made little difference to their financial position. To modern eyes, wages at this time seem pitifully meagre but it must be remembered that the Scottish economy was still firmly based on the land. In small burghs like Largs the householder would have his own piece of ground where he could cultivate a modest crop, grow vegetables and fruit for his own use, keep a few hens and perhaps a pig. More than likely he would also have the right to pasture a cow on the common grazing ground. The landowners had their home farms, and even the minister, working his glebe, was a part-time farmer. Money was required only for things that could not be produced at home.

Those who could neither work the land nor earn money, and whose families were unable to support them, were the responsibility of the Church. Funds for poor relief were raised largely from church door offerings and for these the congregation required small sums of money.

That the thrifty collected false and foreign coins for an ultimate destination in the church plate is proved by cashbooks from some churches where the amount of the weekly collection is entered as "in good copper". Not that the rejects were wasted. They could be gathered until there was a sufficient quantity to be sold for scrap metal. The Poor Fund would probably be kept in a stout chest with two locks: the two separate keys held by the treasurer and another elder so that neither could open it without the presence and co-operation of his fellow "box master".

Care for the deserving poor of the parish was accepted as desirable and humane but it required discrimination, for claimants were many and could at times be unscrupulous. The church door collections provided the main source of the funds and, even though it was not unknown for elders to call on infrequent church attenders for the purpose of uplifting their offerings, the total sum remained small. If necessary it could be supplemented from the heritors by additional contributions which were supposedly voluntary but certainly unpopular. Some such assessment probably explains a document drawn up at the

"Kirktown of Largs September 23d, 1725. The which day David Boyl, Earl of Glasgow, John Lord Boyl his eldest son and Hugh Montgomerie of Hartfield having met to consider an Act of the Justices of the Shire of Air for the charitable relieving of Indigent Poor People who are the real objects of Christian Charity within the bounds of the Parish of Largs and for preventing the burden and oppression the said Parish suffers by idle and masterful Beggars who frequently travel in numbers thro' the sd Parish. They do in the First Place earnestly recommend to the Rev. Mr Andrew Cumine minister of the sd Parish of Largs and the Kirk Session with all convenient diligence to call in any arents that may happen to be resting of the mortified Money destined for the use of the Poor of the said Parish who having orderly considered the arent arising from the mortified money with the weekly collections for the Poor of the sd Parish may further if need be's lay on upon the valuation of the sd Parish such a summ as may. Partually serve to relieve their own Poor. And to prevent in all time coming the

Burden and Oppression the Parish may suffer by idle and masterful Beggars travelling amongst them. They hereby give express order to the Officers of the Laird of Hartfield, the Laird of Brisbane and the Earl of Glasgow and John Burns Beddal of the said Parish whom we nominate and appoint Constables for that effect to apprehend the persons of any such idle and masterful Beggars and carry them straight to the Magistrates of the Town of Air to be received and employed by them as the several Acts of Parliament and Proclaimation of Council do direct. And do also earnestly recommend to the sd Rev. Andrew Cumine and the session if there be any money in hand belonging to the Poor of the Said Parish that they at Martinmas at Furdest lend out the money for arent together with the bygone arents that may be resting of the mortified money foresd that we may have the clear state of the fund before us at our next meeting. In witness whereof thir presents written by Mr Patrick Tweed, schoolmaster at Largs, Day and Date subscribed by Glasgow

       Boyle
       Hugh Montgomerie".

  The "constables" appointed were known locally as "Buff the Beggars", and it was their duty to eject intinerant beggars from the parish so that the Session's resources could be husbanded for the benefit of the local poor. To this end the capital in the Poor Fund was used to purchase "two ground annuals lying near to the Cross of the City of Glasgow"; the Largs poor being "entitled to the said rents from Whitsunday last 1731". The business was managed by "a Glasgow writer named John Robertson" who had "much trouble and pains" over the transaction and for whose legal expertise the Session expressed their grateful thanks.

  The "mortified money" or "mortifications" were sums bequeathed to the Session for the benefit of the Poor Fund. Between Martinmas 1701 and Martinmas 1760 Lady Bishoptown bequeathed 100 merks to the poor; and a certain Major James Milliken donated £20, this generosity being explained by the gloss "his mother a native". There were also accrued to the fund £105:11s being stipend due to Mr John Wilson "minister of bygone". Though there is no actual proof that this was the Rev. John Wilson who died unmarried in 1699, it does look like a final settlement of his estate. In addition, Christina Paton "gave into the session her haill stock" amounting to £7: 7s: 0d. "upon condition of her being alimented". It would appear from the scanty records that over the period covered voluntary contributions amounted in all to £177: 6s: 10d.

The surviving records show that the Largs congregation was not unduly poor and could be generous. Loans and grants were made to parishioners for a great variety of reasons and in 1730 a contribution was sent to provide comforts for poor fishermen's children in Banff and Anstruther; victims perhaps of some east coast tragedy. The Session also made itself responsible for contributing towards the education of those scholars in the parish school whose parents could not afford the fees.

Patrick Tweed had succeeded William Young, who died in retirement in West Kilbride in 1727, as parochial schoolmaster and, as usual, he acted also as Session Clerk. Some of his receipts survived:

> "1728. Received from Theophilus Rankine 2 sh. stg. as my Clerk's salary due from Whitsunday 1727 to Whitsunday 1728 and from 1728 to 1729. Sgd Patrick Tweed"
>
> "Largs June 2nd 1733. D. Sat. I have received from Theophilus Rankine, Kirk Treasurer, under my salary as Clerk and Poor scholars wages from Whitsunday 1729 to Whitsunday 1733. Patrick Tweed"

Unfortunately, in the second entry the total was not entered, but the Session did keep a careful watch over the school accounts for in 1743 Patrick Tweed's receipt for £18: 6s. as "Poor Scholars Wages" had been annotated by the schoolmaster:

> "N.B. Some of the Elders objected against Robt Leitch, which is excepted out of the above account so that I received only Seventeen pound fourteen shillings".

Theophilus Rankine, the treasurer, was a blacksmith to trade – one is tempted to hope not also a locksmith. His wife was Jean Wilson and his rather unusual Christian name was for several generations common locally in the Rankine and Tyre families.

Information about Largs Church during Andrew Cumin's long ministry can be deduced from the general historical background. Until well into the 18th century the principal city churches were alone in having pews. In country kirks there was inevitable confusion as the congregation competed for a wall to lean against as they stood, or for a favourite place on which to deposit the "creepie" stools they brought with them. This turmoil did not always cease when the service started, for the General Assembly issued instructions to "persons of all classes" to refrain from "entertaining one another with discourses while divine worship was performing"; from engaging in disputes that led to brawls; and in extreme cases, from casting divots at each other. It would be too optimistic to assume that the worshippers in Largs were any better than their neighbours and that the Poor Fund did not occasionally benefit from fines imposed for disorderly conduct in church. In an attempt to improve the standard of praise, the Assembly had also instructed that all parochial schoolmasters should be able to teach the psalm tunes. Almost certainly Patrick Tweed had satisfied the minister and Kirk Session as to his proficiency in the twelve common tunes of the Scottish Church but it is impossible to say how effective his instruction was.

Outwith the church, too, there was work to be done. When a poor man's daughter was married, friends and neighbours often contributed to the cost of the celebrations. Alarmed by the excessive drinking and immorality that frequently accompanied these "penny weddings", the church courts ordered ministers and elders to make every effort to ensure that numbers and behaviour were kept within reasonable limits at such festivities. In 1724 Largs, like other churches, would receive a directive from the Synod of Glasgow regarding the duties of elders.

It laid down that they must daily conduct family prayers in their own homes both morning and evening; they must diligently attend all Kirk Session Meetings and the Presbytery when so appointed; they must carefully observe the people in their districts and visit them twice yearly to encourage them in private worship and to help them to recognise their shortcomings if they came under scandal; they must visit the sick regularly to converse and pray with them; and finally, they must "with all zeal and tenderness" reprove the offences of those with whom they came into ordinary daily contact. The eldership was no sinecure and, at least in theory, it was held to have an important influence on the ethics of the whole community.

From 1706 to 1710 David Boyle of Kelburn represented the Queen as Royal High Commissioner at the General Assembly. One can imagine Andrew Cumin setting out for the Assembly in these years in his "braws", his wig well dressed and surmounted by the cocked hat that was the symbol of his dignity and social position – ordinary folk wore bonnets – and no doubt with a list of small purchases to be made in the city, of household necessities and childish trifles not readily available in Largs. The colleagues he met on the journey and with whom he forgathered in Edinburgh would probably treat him with some deference. As parish minister of the Lord High Commissioner, and as the former tutor to his family, he could be expected to have the ear of that dignitary and might be persuaded to raise with him matters that his fellow commissioners regarded as important. Yet Andrew Cumin was not always merely to bask in reflected glory. On at least two subsequent occasions he was to make his mark on the Assembly in his own right.

In 1712, without consultation, Parliament reimposed the right of lay patrons to select parish ministers. The Act was bitterly resented as State interference in congregational authority and it was to have far-reaching effects on the subsequent history of the Scottish Church. In general, the patron was the most important local landowner but in some parishes rival lairds disputed over their boasted rights of patronage and attempted to secure them in long-standing feuds. Nor was it unusual for an acknowledged patron to present his favoured preacher to a charge only to find that the Presbytery was unwilling to induct him or that the congregation had locked church and manse against him. The patron's nominee might well be forced to take possession of his church by climbing through the window or to arrive in the parish with a military escort prepared to quell incipient riot. Largs was, however, spared the disgraceful scenes that occurred elsewhere, for whatever people thought about patronage it never became an active issue.

For one thing, in 1712 the minister of Largs, Andrew Cumin, was a young man and the question of appointing a successor to him was not to arise for many years. Moreover, there was no dissension as to the legal patron. In 1587 the last Commendator of Paisley Abbey, Lord Claud Hamilton, was created Lord Paisley and granted by the Crown all the property of the Abbey. On his death in 1621, these holdings passed to his grandson the second Earl of Abercorn, who soon afterwards openly declared himself to be a Catholic and left the country. In 1652 he sold the lordship of Paisley to the Earl of Angus, who in the following year sold it to Lord Cochrane, afterwards Earl of Dundonald. The patronage of Largs Church conformed to this general pattern. In March 1591/2 the Charter to Lord Claud Hamilton of the abbacy of Paisley included the Church of Largs; in 1647 negotiations regarding the division of the parish were made with Lord Abercorn and in 1671, when the stipend was diverted for charitable purposes, it was with the Earl of Dundonald that the arrangements were made.

Soon after this the patronage of Largs Church was acquired by the Montgomeries of Skelmorlie and through them it passed by inheritance in 1735 to the Montgomeries of Coilsfield and later to their descendants the Earls of Eglinton, with whom it remained until the final abolition of lay patronage in 1874.

Although other principles were involved, patronage was the overt cause of the series of secessions from the Established Church in the 18th and 19th centuries. The first came in 1733 when, under the leadership of the Rev. Ebenezer Erskine, Minister of Stirling, four ministers – the number later increased to eight – maintained the rights of congregations to choose their own ministers and formed themselves into a separate Presbytery though they continued to carry out their parochial duties.

There was considerable sympathy for their opinions, but widespread fear that their intransigence threatened the hard-won unity of the national Church. They were allowed to retain their churches, manses, and stipends; and efforts were made to reach a compromise with them. It was not until 1740 that a motion to depose them came before the General Assembly. Andrew Cumin was one of those who counselled moderation and who, after the Act expelling them had been passed, had their dissent from the majority decision minuted. The dissenting clergymen formed their own "Associate Synod" outside of the Established Church and some 40 Secession congregations were formed, mostly in small towns. Andrew Cumin's tolerant belief that the Church should be able to accept divergent views was perhaps the reason why no Secession

Church was set up in Largs for many years.

In 1742 Andrew Cumin came second in the voting when the General Assembly elected the Rev. George Logan of Trinity College, Edinburgh as its Moderator. It was the nearest Largs has ever come to providing a Moderator for the General Assembly and is some indication of the esteem in which his colleagues held this elderly parish minister. But Cumin's ministry in Largs had lasted for forty years, and in May 1742 he handed over his active duties to his son, John.

JOHN CUMIN

John Cumin was born in 1714. After studying at the University of Glasgow he was licensed by the Presbytery of Irvine on 5th June 1739, and was ordained assistant and successor to his father on 27th May, 1742. Andrew Cumin's was the longest recorded ministry in Largs; his son's was to be the shortest, for John Cumin died on 31st January 1743, after only eight months in the charge Andrew Cumin resumed sole responsibility for the parish in an unsettled time.

There were echoes of foreign war and rebellion at home and, though Largs was not directly affected by the Jacobite Rising of 1745, two surviving records give some suggestion of disturbed local conditions:

"Nov. 12th 1745. To a lame soldier for lodging and carrying to Kilbryde one pound eighteen shillings Scots".

"Dec. 13th 1745. To thirteen poor sailors ten shillings by order of the Session".

Another brief note indicates one way in which the Kirk Session's charity was financed:

"10 shillings Scots, the charge of ringing the bell on the occasion of a funeral".

There were proposals for change within the Church itself but little evidence that these were implemented. In 1745 a book of metrical paraphrases was published and the General Assembly approved its use in public worship. But even if the Largs congregation had ever heard of it, few country kirks considered even for a moment the introduction of these human compositions alongside the Psalms of David. One piece of legislation passed in the wake of the Jacobite Rising had indirect effects on the Church. The Burgess Oath was an affirmation of loyalty to the State required in certain towns from all who held public office, even quite minor posts. It was intended as a safeguard against Jacobite sympathisers but it had an even greater influence on the Secession Church. Many of the Seceders believed that the oath implied an allegiance to the Established Church that they were not prepared to give, and as a result the Secession Church split into two: those who refused to take the oath became known as "Anti-Burghers", and formed an independent "General Associate Synod", thus cutting themselves off not only from the existing Secession Church but also from all participation in public affairs. On the other hand, the Associate Synod, or "Burghers", held that it was quite permissible to give an undertaking that they would not openly oppose the Established Church although they were not themselves committed to that communion.

The second part of Andrew Cumin's ministry lasted for six years but in 1748, when he must have been in his seventies, he again handed over his duties to a young colleague.

PATRICK WALLACE

Patrick Wallace was the son of the Rev. Archibald Wallace, minister of Cardross, who died in 1725, leaving a widow and eight children. McGregor's *History of Glasgow* notes:

> "In October, 1728, an interesting appointment was made. The Town Council then approved of a contract between the magistrates and Susannah Smith, widow of the late Rev. Archibald Wallace, minister of Cardross, by which Mrs Wallace was nominated mistress of the public school erected in the city for teaching girls "to spin flax into fine yarn fit for making thread or cambrick." The lady was to receive an annual "encouragement" of £30 sterling, granted by the Commissioners and Trustees of the Improvement of Fisheries and Manufactories in Scotland."

The salary proved sufficiently encouraging for Susannah Wallace to bring up and educate her four sons and four daughters. Patrick, the third son, graduated at Glasgow University in 1736 and was licensed by the Presbytery of Irvine on 10th August, 1742. In March 1748, Largs Church represented to the Presbytery that he had "several times preached amongst them to their great satisfaction", and had "piety, prudence, literature and other good ministerial qualities". He was called to Largs on 31st March 1748, with the good wishes of the patron, the Earl of Glasgow; Brisbane; Blair of Blair; and "other powerful men of the neighbourhood"; and was ordained and inducted as the second assistant and successor to Andrew Cumin.

Patrick Wallace remains a shadowy figure in the list of local ministers. In his time, musical enthusiasts were carrying praise far beyond the twelve tunes commonly used in the Scottish Church. Whether the minister and precentor in Largs had any success in overcoming conservative prejudices and teaching the new tunes, or even whether they had any wish to do so, is not known. Possibly Patrick Wallace was more interested in the unavailing attempts being made to increase Church stipends. They could be as little as £30 per year, the majority being between £40 and £70, with an average of about £52. About 100 ministers received between £70 and £100, while only a handful reached the astounding heights of a three figure stipend. Largs was relatively fortunate with a stipend of £72: 3s: 4d. per year and the minister was a wealthy man compared to the parochial schoolmaster, Patrick Tweed, whose tiny salary had to be eked out by the small fees paid by his pupils and a pittance as Session Clerk. Theophilus Rankine had ceased to be kirk treasurer by 25th October 1750, when the receipt that Patrick Tweed signed for his poor scholars' fees was made out to William Blair, Treasurer and keeper of the Mortcloths. Tweed received the sum of £11: 14s. Scots due for seven pupils.

Patrick Wallace's ministry was short: sadly short in view of the sacrifices that attended his education for it. He died, unmarried, on 18th November 1755. By that time the aged Andrew Cumin, in the fifty-fourth year of his ministry, could no longer be expected to take over the active duties of the parish and within the year his third assistant, Gilbert Lang, was appointed

GILBERT LANG

Gilbert Lang, the son of Andrew Lang "sclater" in Greenock and Jean Moor, was born on the 1st of January 1725, and baptised two days later. Educated at Glasgow University, he was ordained and inducted as assistant and successor to Andrew Cumin on 3rd April, 1756. For six years Cumin remained officially minister of Largs but on 4th July 1762, he died "Father of the Church" in the 61st year of his ministry at the age of 88, and Gilbert Lang assumed sole responsibility for the parish.

A new manse was built in 1762 beside the glebe in the South Kirklands. Two years later the former manse "being in great disrepair" was sold for £64 to Archibald Frazer, wright and mason in Largs. Including Gilbert Lang himself for a brief period, sixteen successive parish ministers had lived and worked in the old house since the Reformation and perhaps several priests before them. The key of the main door, over five inches in length with a shaft rounded at the point but a square handle, is still preserved in the custody of the minister.

Yet the old manse had not outlived its usefulness. Subdivided into separate dwellings with forestairs, it continued to be inhabited for more than a century until in 1900 it was demolished and the present tenement block was built on its site in Manse Court.

It was to the new manse that Gilbert Lang brought his wife, when on 18th November 1765 he married Eupham, daughter of Patrick Maxwell, minister of Inchinnan. Their daughter, Janet, was born on 15th August and died on 20th October, 1767, and Eupham Lang herself died on 7th November, 1768. On 5th February 1771, Gilbert Lang married again; this time to D'Arcy Miller, daughter of Thomas Miller, who was employed on the Brisbane Estate and who presumably had his daughter baptised in compliment to the laird's family, where D'Arcy was a Christian name. According to local tradition D'Arcy Miller was in service at Brisbane House. It was there that the minister became attracted to the pretty housemaid and the unusual marriage raised eyebrows and caused no little sensation in the district. Yet it seems to have worked out remarkably well. Gilbert Lang always spoke with the greatest affection of his young wife and she apparently adapted herself rapidly to her changed position.

The new manse was described as having been built "on spacious lines"; it was just as well, for soon it was crowded with young Langs:

    Jean, born 12th May 1772, died 1785
    D'Arcy, born 2nd March, 1776
    Elizabeth, born 14th December, 1777
    Andrew, born 28th September, 1779
    Margaret, born 27th August, 1781
    Isabella, born 3rd May, 1783, died 2nd January, 1824
    Gilbert, born 22nd June, 1784
    John, born 4th and died 8th March, 1786
    Patrick, born 17th November, 1787
    Thomas, born 1st April, 1788 [*sic*]
    Mary, born 9th April, 1789
    John, born 2nd March, 1791[19]

By Gilbert Lang's time the picture of the Parish of Largs is becoming clearer. A few miscellaneous Church papers are extant and some accounts of Lang have survived in the folk memory of the place. It is recalled that Gilbert Lang preached "a memorable series of sermons" on the twelve texts in the decoration of the ceiling of the Skelmorlie Aisle. It was also said, "Mr Lang wrote a very pretty hand, but evidently he was sparing of his paper". Paper was certainly expensive, but that no one could have accused Gilbert Lang of being spendthrift was proved by a sermon on the sixth chapter of St John's Gospel which survived into the 20th century. It consisted of some 4,000 words written beautifully and – for those with eyesight equal to the task – quite legibly on a piece of paper no bigger than a postcard.

At this time people were forming voluntary associations for various purposes and Lang was probably called upon to conduct the service when, on 21st December 1767, the Largs Masonic Lodge was founded.

John, third Earl of Glasgow, represented the King as Lord High

Commissioner to the General Assembly from 1764 to 1772. He was a great favourite there

> "not only for his obliging manners and improved entertainment, but for his attention to the business of the House, and his listening to and entering into the spirit of every debate".

Once again as this dignitary's parish minister, the Largs minister would be a person of some consequence at the Assembly and Gilbert Lang preached there in 1765, as he had already done in 1758.

By far the most detailed description of 18th century Largs appears in the *Statistical Account of Scotland*. Sir John Sinclair, a prominent agriculturalist and economist, conceived the idea of producing a comprehensive record of social conditions throughout Scotland. He prevailed upon the parish ministers each to write a report on his own district, covering certain specified topics and adding any other material that seemed of interest. Gilbert Lang completed his survey of the Parish of Largs in 1790 and it was printed in one of the early volumes of Sinclair's work. Soon after its publication, a second report on Largs appeared with the explanation that the original

> "being rather short and defective, the valuable addition to it, herewith printed, was sent by an intelligent and respectable friend to this great undertaking".

The intelligent and respectable person remains anonymous. He wrote in 1794 and added a good deal of detail – not always accurate – so that the two reports together give a very full account of Largs. Lang's article was certainly short but the criticism of it is often repeated without question, somewhat unfairly.

The great value of *The Statistical Account* is that it gives a comprehensive description of the 938 parishes in Scotland at a time when the whole way of Scottish life was changing, but before the full impact of the agrarian and industrial revolutions had taken effect.

Yet it has another almost equally important function. It gives a survey of the interests, enthusiasms and, indeed, eccentricities of the parish ministers who played such an influential part in the local communities. So far as Largs is concerned, for the very first time it allows the minister to communicate directly with succeeding generations.

Looking back over almost thirty-five years, Lang took a long-term and inherently tolerant view of Largs. His comments on its history and antiquities are those to be expected from any reasonably well-informed person of the time; but he did coin two quite memorable phrases. With regard to the isolation of Largs he quotes a saying "Out of Scotland into Largs"; and he maintains that, because of its temperate climate, Largs was often described as "the Montpelier of Scotland". These observations were to become the platitudes of 19th century descriptions in guide books of Largs.

The population of the parish was estimated in 1756 as 1,164 inhabitants, about half resident in the town itself. This made Largs a not inconsiderable place in view of the fact that Kilmarnock, the biggest town in Ayrshire, had then a population of hardly more than 4,000. Lang pointed out that in more recent years "the population of the country part of the parish has certainly decreased; but the town of Largs ... has proportionally increased" due, the additional article explained, "to several small farms being comprehended in greater ones, and a number evacuated to enlarge the plantation at Kelburn". There is little other reference to the new methods of agriculture which, elsewhere in Ayrshire, were making sweeping changes. Apart from the town of Largs, the only other real concentration of people in the parish was on its southern boundary at Fairlie, where there were something under 300 inhabitants. Skelmorlie, in the north, was recognised as a separate entity though its inhabitants were widely scattered.

Lang saw the local people as:
> "in general quiet, sober, decent, people. Living chiefly among themselves, they are strangers, and so far, perhaps, happy strangers, to the more free and licentious manners of the world around them".

Perhaps because he regarded all his parishioners as of equal importance, he saw no need to specify any by name. However, the writer of the second part listed the chief proprietors in the parish as:
> "the Earl of Glasgow, Thomas Brisbane of Brisbane, Colonel Hugh Montgomery of Skelmurly, William Blair of Blair, and Thomas King of Blackhouse, besides William Wilson of Hailley, and Daniel Fraser of

Hangenheugh, who hold of the family of Brisbane, and thirteen feuers upon the estate of Brisbane".

With regard to public health, he observed that the local people were so remarkably healthy that "medical assistance was seldom necessary". Nevertheless, he found a few examples of longevity. In Largs at the time of writing, William Crawford was aged 86 and James Martin 85, while Robert Adam of Kipping-burn was 84 and Alexander Blair of Outer-wards was 87. The most outstanding example of long life was James Hendry, who in 1754 had died at Tourgill aged 103; though perhaps the modern reader should add as the Court did in 1648, "or thereby".

Out of a total of 126 tradesmen enumerated by Lang, no less than 66 were weavers "employed by the manufacturers of Paisley, who have been of great benefit to the place". The other craftsmen were the scattering of carpenters, tailors, smiths, coopers, masons and so on, required to provide the services necessary in the community. Fishing, Lang concluded, had been "much less attended to than it ought to be". Both writers comment on what must have been the most notable annual event:

"There is in Largs a weekly market on Thursdays, and four annual fairs, the most remarkable of which is St Columba's day, vulgarly called Comb's day ... . This fair is famous over the west of Scotland, and continues from Monday to Thursday. Great numbers of people, from 40 to 50 miles round, resort to it, some for business and some for pleasure. Upwards of 100 boats are often to be seen, on this occasion, riding in the Bay. They spend the whole night in rustic sports, carousing and dancing on the green to the sound of the bagpipes".

Gilbert Lang viewed the festivities with an almost unexpectedly kindly eye:

"The spectacle of boats from all quarters, the crowds of people, the sound of music; ashore dancing and hilarity, day and night on the green; and further up a new street, or town, formed of the stands of merchants, and filled with a press of people, formed altogether an amusing spectacle".

Colm's Fair had originally been intended to provide an opportunity for trade between the Highlands and the Lowlands but it is quite an interesting point that in the late 18th century both reporters were of the opinion that it was already on the decline.

Fundamental changes in the Largs way of life were foreshadowed. As early as 1790 Lang could write that Largs "has been frequented a good deal of late, in the summer months, by many persons and families, for the sake of health or amusement; and it would be still more, if there were better accommodation"

But it was not only poor accommodation that deterred visitors. Largs was not an easy place to reach.

In Scotland the main public roads were the responsibility of the Commissioners of Supply, who were drawn from the landed classes. All able-bodied men within any parish were required by law to give a specified number of hours' work on the roads, though this could be commuted to a money payment for the hire of labourers.

The regulations were often ignored and even at best the Statute Labour increasingly proved quite inadequate for anything like a reasonable standard of maintenance. In south Ayrshire, Lord Cathcart proposed early in the 18th century to provide carts free to his tenants. The offer was promptly declined on the grounds that the state of the roads rendered wheeled vehicles quite useless. The first Turnpike Act in Ayrshire was passed in 1767, empowering trustees to raise money by loans, by commutation of Statute Labour, and by tolls. Gradually the condition of Ayrshire roads began to improve.

The main road from Glasgow to Port Patrick ran the length of the parish of Largs. What the 17th century had considered impossible, was achieved when the first bridge over the Gogo was built in 1724. The Noddle Bridge soon followed. Largs was no longer cut off when the burns were in spate and a few years later a new road from Skelmorlie was built along the shore to replace the former more difficult route on higher ground. A road, privately maintained, led from Largs to Brisbane House, but these were the only two roads in the parish. However, as in the rest of Scotland, numerous well-defined tracks connected centres of population. Little more than footpaths, they could be used by riders on horseback; but supplies and produce could be conveyed along them only in the small loads that could be carried by packhorses. There were proposals to extend the Brisbane Road to Kilmacolm and to build a road to Kilbirnie and Dalry; but to the end of the 18th century these remained talk, without even reaching the planning stage.

The Reids are the first family known to have spent a holiday in

Largs. The youngest son, Robert, lived to be a very old man and in his later years wrote a description of the summer he spent in Largs as a ten year old.[20] His account of the journey gives some indication of the stamina required from prospective visitors. John Reid, a wealthy Glasgow merchant, rented Haylie House – a predecessor of the present building – for the season of 1782 at a cost of £5. Having negotiated the lease, his obligations were at an end and it fell to his wife Elizabeth to arrange the whole process of transporting the family to their "salt-water quarters". To this end she hired one James Neilson and his Paisley caravan – from the context this would appear to have been a capacious covered-wagon of the type familiar in western films. On the appointed day it drew up outside the Reid home in the Candlerigs and into it were loaded Elizabeth Reid, her nine children, three maid servants – one suffering from a new-fangled sickness "which had just got the name of influenza" – and the vast amount of impedimenta necessary to make life tolerable in a place like Largs. They crossed Glasgow Bridge and plodded along the leafy lanes of Kingston, eventually arriving in the late afternoon at Kilbirnie. There the horse was seized by a mysterious illness, which seems to have been not unconnected with its owner's discovery that there was no road to Largs. The party spent the night at the Kilbirnie inn, but in the morning James Neilson flatly refused to go any further. He would not, he stated firmly, be responsible for the lives of the children on the wastes ahead. Two strong country carts were hired; the travellers and their goods were stowed into them and they set off on the last perilous eight miles of their journey. Robert Reid wrote that it was soon apparent that

"James Neilson was not far wrong in refusing to risk his caravan upon this muir-road, for it was just a track of deep mud-holes, slippery rocks, and loose stones and boulders. In some parts it was very steep and undoubtedly dangerous; in fact it required the strictest attention of our new carters to keep the carts from being capsized. The country farmers who had occasion to lead peats from this muir at the period in question used sledges with long trams, which are not easily overturned".

It must have been with no little sense of relief that the Reids finally reached their destination. It was not, of course, to be supposed that John Reid could absent himself from his important business

The Old Manse was a typical small town house of the 17th century. The door on the left was the entrance to the stable and the upper right window overlooking the graveyard was said to have been the minister's study. The photograph shows the house after the church had disposed of it and it had been divided into separate dwellings.

commitments in the city for the whole summer nor that he would undergo the inconveniences of his wife's method of transport. He remained in Glasgow until his family had settled into their temporary dwelling and prepared it suitably for his reception. He then paid occasional visits, adopting the "comfortable plan" of taking a seat on the stage-coach to Greenock. The fare was 5s 6d and the coach stopped at Bishopton to give the passengers time to dine. At Greenock he hired a horse and a boy was sent to walk across the moor by a short cut so that he could receive the horse at Largs and ride it back to its home stable.

As a little boy, Robert Reid was naturally more interested in the holiday activities than in the place itself. But his reminiscences do add something to the description of Largs:

"The lodging-houses were all small, most of them merely single rooms, and none of them self-contained. The inhabitants of Largs had not yet learned to turn the penny by letting lodgings, and seemed to regard with the utmost indifference any applications by our Glasgow folks for furnished apartments; indeed they appeared to consider it a favour to give up any part of their own houses to strangers".

Living at Haylie House, the Reids saw little enough of the town, though Robert Reid does in retrospect make a few comments on it. There is a rather mysterious reference to

"one person who was called 'the Laird' who had his dwelling near the thorn tree which stood in the middle of the main street".

The town was a "primitive-looking place" with most of the houses thatched and scarcely any of them fronted the sea. The Broomfields were then "in a state of nature, and covered with whins; among which were many cairns". The whole area of the foreshore was known as "the Common of Largs" and the only building on it was Lord Bute's coach-house and stables, where he left his carriage and horses when he crossed to Mount Stuart. It was on the site where the Brisbane Centre now stands.

When the Reids came to leave Largs at the end of the summer it is not surprising that there was no further mention of the Paisley caravan. Instead, Elizabeth Reid

"engaged the Largs packet, which brought us all up to Glasgow, after a fine passage of twelve hours".

Setting aside the disadvantage that it was impossible to estimate how long a journey by sailing ship would take, there was no doubt that, except in the stormiest weather, it was much less wearing to travel by sea than by land. Countless small boats darted around the Firth and most were prepared to take passengers. Freight was brought into Largs by the sloop "Brisbane of Largs". The skipper was Robbie Hunter, who could usually be relied on to accomplish the round trip to Glasgow within the week. When, as often happened, he was grounded on one of the shifting sandbanks that impeded navigation in the upper reaches of the river, he accepted the position philosophically and waited until the rising tide floated him off. Since there was no pier at Largs, his practice was to sail the "Brisbane of Largs" into the mouth of the Gogo at high water. The ebbing tide beached her and the cargo was manhandled ashore.

Both contributors to the Statistical Account extol the splendid anchorage in the Fairlie Roads. It was "a bay that would contain any number of ships, sheltered from every storm" and "vessels of any burthen may ride in it at all seasons, and loose from it with any wind". On the journey to Largs two centuries ago, the little Robert Reid looked down with admiration, as people still do today, from the summit of Auchenbranchen Hill:

> "Here the beautiful view of the firth broke upon us, with the islands of Cumbrae, Bute and Arran lying expanded right in our front, and three or four fine ships resting at anchor in the Fairlie Roads. At the lapse of seventy years I still remember with pleasure the first impression of this enchanting scene; for the ships viewed from the heights, seemed to me as small as my own toy ships, and the sea between Largs and Cumbrae appeared like a fine pool of water".

Ocean-going ships could sail as far up the Clyde as Greenock but many chose not to do so. In port, merchant seamen were a prey to naval press gangs and this was especially so in Greenock during the War of American Independence. It was not unknown for ships' masters to anchor in Fairlie Roads and pay off most of the crew. The ship, manned by captain, mate, and apprentices, could sail up the Firth, discharge its cargo, re-load and, outward bound, pick up the rest of the crew by previous arrangement. This manoeuvre had the added advantage that customs officials were likely to be less efficiently organised at Fairlie than they were at Greenock.

"There is," Gilbert Lang wrote, "no smuggling worth the mentioning". However, he did betray his own sympathies when he added "unless the pitiful and occasional help given to the poor seamen, in their little adventures, can be called such". Yet an extract from the Custom House Books of Irvine shows that some of the "quiet, sober, decent, people" of Largs had nothing to learn in the way of double-crossing, compounding felonies, and dealing with venal officials:

> "Oath of Robert Thompson, 23rd Feb. 1765. – Robert Thompson, vintner at Fairlie, maketh oath that in the month of Feb 1763, there came into Largs a wherry from the Isle of Man, laden with about five or six hundred casks of brandy and rum the whole of which were landed there, when Archd. Stewart, officer of Excise at Largs, was coming and going upon the shore; that before the goods were landed, he, Mr Stewart, compounded with ——
> ——, farmer in Largs, and others then present, for 18 casks of the same, which he the deponent delivered to Mr Stewart with his own hands, when he told him that 9 of which were for the king, and the other 9 for himself, and which 18 casks he, Mr Stewart, delivered to John Craig, cooper in

Largs, who carried off and lodged them in the Excise office there, when Mr Stewart stayed and saw the residue of the cargo carried off. That, at same time, the deponent heard Mr Stewart say, that he nor no other Excise officer should trouble the people that were concerned in the cargo for 2 or 3 days. Robert Thompson, vintner, Fairlie, being further examined, maketh oath that one day, when Mr Stewart, Excise officer at Largs, was drinking in the deponent's house, he heard him, the said Stewart, say, when talking about compositions in general, that William Knox, tidesman, had no power to make compositions, as he and the rest of the Excisemen had, and further maketh oath, that he has frequently heard Mr Stewart speak of a power that Excisemen were invested with to compound with the smugglers. The Collector and Comptroller report that when examining Thompson and other witnesses, Stewart the Excise officer appeared with a notary public demanding to be present at the examination, which they refused – he protesting against their doing so".

The detailed description of 18th century Largs sets the scene in which Gilbert Lang lived and worked. The rising standard of living is reflected in his emoluments: he began his ministry with a stipend of £72:3s:4d but before its close the figure had risen to £124: 12s: 6d. Yet in his later years he was no longer the only minister in Largs. A group of people who had been travelling fourteen miles to Greenock to attend public worship and receive the sacraments presented a "petition for sermon" to the Burgher Presbytery of Glasgow, which on 13th April 1779 appointed a Greenock minister to preach at Largs from time to time. Services were held in a tent on the Greenhill or in Gogo Mill until in the following year a small meeting-house was built in Waterside Street "at a cost of £167: 5s: 7d. and 4s 2d more". By 1783 the congregation was sufficiently strong to call a permanent minister of its own and ten years later the supplementary report in the Statistical Account records:

"The greater number of the inhabitants are of the Established Church. About fifty families are Burghers; and, to the honour of both parties, they live together in mutual amity, without exhibiting, in almost any instance, the smallest alienation of affection on account of different religious sentiments".

Yet the Established Church remained solely responsible for social welfare and had to expend energy and income on its obligations to the community as a whole. As late as 1794, church door offerings amounted only to £40 in the year. In 1788, John Morrice of Craig, Esq., "who was born in this parish, and acquired an opulent fortune

in the West Indies" left £50 to the poor; and the late Countess Dowager of Glasgow
"with that humanity and goodness which so eminently distinguished her character, when she left this parish in 1775 upon the death of her Lord, ordered £10 per annum to be distributed at the discretion of the minister".

In 1794 there were 20 people on the poor relief list of the parish receiving sums varying from one guinea to £4 annually; three regular pensioners received 2s 6d weekly; and there were, besides, 21 persons "who receive small sums as their exigiencies require". Some of the casual charitable outlays appear in copies of instructions sent to William Blair, the Kirk Treasurer, by Gilbert Lang:
"William, Give Susan D. on account of her father, eighteenpence, and mark it in your book."
"William, you may give a shilling to this woman from Beith, who is taken ill with a flux here."
"William, Give the Bearer of this two shillings and sixpence, and mark it in your book."

"William" was succeeded as Treasurer by John Greg, some of whose disbursements survive in less explicit detail. In 1787 an unspecified amount was given to "a distressed Sailor by a line from Mr Lang" and in the same year another petitioner rather mysteriously received "Half his Herd's fee", while – in the absence of a national health service – in October 1789, five shillings was
"given to Dr King by Mr Lang's advice for mending James Bog's daughters arm".

In a seaside parish there were sometimes expenses that could not be avoided. In May 1787, the sum of 19s 7d. had to be disbursed
"for Expences for Coffing, Bell and other expenses for a cart and going to Skelmorly shore and Intertanin the popel attending the Corpe borne in at sea to Largs Churchyeard".

The unknown was not unceremoniously bundled underground, but the considerable outlay for a more seemly disposal of the remains could hardly be criticised since it was from funerals that the poor funds derived a regular additional income.

The parish mortcloth was a large square pall, generally of black velvet bound with silk fringes, used to cover a coffin on its way to the graveyard. In William Blair's time the fee for hiring the mortcloth was twelve shillings, but in most parishes there were also less elaborate mortcloths, of plush perhaps or even coarse black cloth, which could serve the function of decently covering the coffin with greater economy. In Largs, references to the mortcloth are usually made in the plural so that there does seem to have been a choice; though the use of one or other of the official mortcloths was obligatory and could easily be enforced since a refusal to dig the grave could speedily bring the independently minded bereaved to a more conformist attitude. The Kirk Session jealously guarded its monopoly on the use of the official mortcloths not only because of the income that accrued from them, but also because there were misguided persons who might use some unsuitable covering as a pall, perhaps even one with an embroidered cross, which to the 18th century would certainly savour of undesirable Popish practices. A receipt shows that the mortcloths were kept in good repair:

"An Account of Mending Mortcloths with thread and linning for the Session of Largs at sundrie times:

To 3 qrs of yard at 4d	1sh.	od.
To mending that cloth		3d.
To 1 yd at 1/4 per yard	1sh.	4d.
To mending 4 cloths with thread...	1sh.	8d.

Thos. Boggs".

·The mortcloths continued in use well into the 19th century. In 1812, perhaps as part of the celebration of the opening of the new church, Mrs John Lade of Noddsdale donated 5 guineas towards the purchase of a new mortcloth, and in 1828 a fresh velvet one was bought at a cost of £21: 10s. In November 1843, Mrs William Duff, widow of the recently deceased Session Clerk, was appointed "Keeper of the Mortcloths", with a commission of 10% on the hiring receipts, and it was not until 1862 that the Session finally disposed of mortcloths and the common kist as no longer required.

In 1801 a hearse was provided for Largs by public subscription. Before that the coffin – or for the very poor the common burial kist – was carried on hand-spokes by bearers. It was one of the duties of the beadle to deliver these, along with trestles and the appropriate mortcloth, to the house from which the funeral would set out.

Previously the bellman on his rounds would have intimated first the death and later the time and place where people should meet "to attend the deceased to the place of burial", for essentially the early funeral was no more than that. The reformed Church had discouraged religious ceremony at funerals in order to avoid the appearance of praying for the dead and this proscription was maintained until well into the 18th century. However, Acts of Parliament laid down certain regulations regarding the use of linen and woollen shrouds and it became necessary to have a responsible person, usually an elder, present at the "kisting" to witness that the law had been duly carried out. In the course of time it became customary to invite the minister also. Since many of the relatives and friends gathered at the house would have travelled considerable distances, some hospitality had to be offered and it was natural that the minister should be asked to say a blessing over the food and drink provided. This gradually developed into a full-scale funeral service before the party set out on foot to carry the coffin to the graveyard.

In the *Largs and Millport Weekly News* in 1906, an account was given of the funeral in 1763 of John Ewing, merchant in Fairlie. David Bryce, who was apparently a local baker, was commissioned to supply

> "buns, short-bread, rolls, and various other requisites, and to bake a cake using the best ingredients which included flour, eggs, butter, sugar, currants, raisins, orange peel, almonds, cloves, carvie seed, grey pepper, cinnamon, and nutmeg".

Altogether the cake sounds more suitable for a wedding than a funeral. Unfortunately, accounts for the drink supplied have not survived; but it must be admitted that when the cortege had to proceed from a remote part of the parish, the refreshment provided en route for bearers and walkers may well have resulted in some of the mourners arriving in the kirkyard in a state of mind hardly suited to the occasion.

Like funerals, christenings and marriages formerly solemnised in church on Sunday came also to be centred on the home. Newly born infants were sadly expendable, and often there was doubt as to whether a sickly child would survive until the following Sunday or would be strong enough to withstand the journey to the church. It became usual for many, perhaps most, baptisms to be conducted by the minister at the child's home and to be followed by such entertainment as the parents thought fitting.

As far as marriages were concerned, the upper classes regarded the often quite lengthy journey to and from the church as a waste of time and indeed the celebrations that followed the ceremony might well be unsuitable on a Sunday. They began to hold weddings on a weekday in their homes and the practice spread until most weddings were solemnised in the home; or if it was too small to accommodate the guests, in some public building. Only the very poor were married in church and then, often, the ceremony took place in the vestry or even in the manse.

Though the church was also responsible for education, funds for the parish school had become "liberal". This had resulted largely from a bequest received about 1760. It was recorded in the following document:

> "Memorandum of Dr Hannibal Hall's Legacie to the Session and School of Largs. Hannibal Hall, a Native born and bred in Largs town, was advanced to be a doctor of medicine in the Town of Dublin, where he died. He left and bequeathed by testament to the parish of Largs for the encouragement of a school in that town the sum of two hundred pound Irish money, and being remitted and sent over from Dublin to the town of Glasgow by an attorney in Dublin by the name Hall, he retained for his pains ten pounds Irish money, the remaining sum was brought to Largs and lent out upon Bond to the magistrates of the town of Irvine at four and a half per cent yearly, and the Bond lodged in the minister of Largs' hands. The which interest in only paid by the said Magistrates of Irvine to the schoolmaster of Largs for the time".

John Dun, who was already schoolmaster when he became Session Clerk in 1791, and John McQueen who succeeded to both offices in 1796, would no doubt welcome the addition to their salaries from the Hannibal Hall Bequest. The annual interest on the legacy of £175 a year figures in the church accounts well into the 19th century. By 1873 the Kirk Session was handing it over to the newly constituted School Board, to whom they made over the full capital some ten years later.

There were, in 1794, between sixty and seventy pupils in the parish school. The quarterly fees for tuition were for reading 1s 6d; for writing 2s; and for arithmetic 2s 6d. Those who aspired to a higher education might also acquire Latin for an additional 3s per quarter. There were in the parish smaller "adventure" schools; so-called because they were run by persons who "adventured" to make a living by instructing pupils privately. Fairlie and Skelmorlie had such schools and probably at various times there were small schools in Largs.

James Greg has been mentioned as Kirk Treasurer. He, like his father before him, was commonly known as "bailie Greg". In early times the superior of the Lordship of Largs held certain legal powers over his vassals. With the passing of the centuries these rights diminished until in 1747 all hereditary jurisdictions were abolished by Act of Parliament. But for more than fifty years Largs retained "Baron-Bailie" as a courtesy title, although James Greg had become in reality no more than the Laird's estate factor. Another kenspeckle figure of the time was William Shearer, the bellman. If later practice is anything to go by, he would combine crying the news with a wide variety of other posts – beadle, sexton, constable, and indeed any semi-official but not over-popular position that fell vacant.

On 11th December 1791, the Parish Register noted "No Sermon, Mr Lang not in health". The same entry was repeated for 18th and 25th December; and under 1st January came the bald announcement
"No Sermon, Mr Lang a corpse, died Freyday last and intered upon Wednesday, 4th 1792".

One of Lang's daughters married a son of Tam Samson, a crony of Robert Burns, and one of his sons attained distinction on Sainte Croix, one of the Virgin Islands, in the consular service of the Danish government. They were a long-lived family with, it was said, at least one golden wedding in every generation. D'Arcy Lang survived her husband by almost half a century. In her later years she lived at Irvine, where she died on 27th August, 1840.

STEPHEN ROWAN

The turn of the century saw a relatively short and uneventful ministry. Stephen Rowan – the name sometimes appears as Rowand – was the son of John Rowan of Glasgow. He was educated at Glasgow University, where he graduated Master of Arts in 1776. Although he was licensed by the Presbytery of Irvine on 28th November 1780, it was not until 8th March 1792 that the patron, Hugh Montgomerie of Coilsfield, presented him as minister to the Church of Largs. He was ordained and inducted on 15th May of the same year. On 27th July 1784, he had married Janet Bogle and they had two children: Janet, born on 28th September 1785; and Stephen born on 26th February, 1787. Stephen Rowan was minister of Largs at a time of national unrest. At war with France, the country had become obsessed by fear of foreign invasion. John Galt in his novel *The Provost* describes the activity in a small Ayrshire town: the address of loyalty to the King; the parish minister's sermon on the need to "arm ourselves in the defence of all that was dear to us"; the public meeting in the church "to take into consideration the best means of saving the King and the kingdom" in the "monstrous crisis of public affairs" and the formation of a volunteer unit for civil defence that became more concerned about its choice of uniform than its professed objective. No doubt Largs reacted in a not dissimilar manner.

In the Church, the 18th century had brought change. As it was established in 1690, the Scottish Church was predominantly puritan; but slowly, and almost imperceptibly, puritanism had declined for various reasons. Civil law no longer endorsed Kirk Session rulings; the Church prided itself on an educated ministry but at the Scottish universities young men were bound to come into contact with more liberal ideas from the Continent; and the Patronage Act had a profound effect. It would perhaps be too severe to describe the parish ministers as the lairds' creatures; but a landed patron was unlikely to select as his nominee any minister who did not accept the prevailing social order, or whose religious convictions were so extreme as to interfere with the comfortable life style of the upper classes. Finally, those ministers and laymen who had a mind for more ascetic religion had an alternative.

Both Burgher and Anti-Burgher Churches maintained the stern old Covenanting beliefs. The Secession had been a middle-class movement, and chiefly lower middle-class. In general, the Seceders were quite ordinary people, though with enough education to have formed their own earnest ideas on the basis of some understanding of the principles involved and with enough money to build simple churches and pay ministers. It is typical that the first trustees of the Largs Burgher congregation included farmers, wrights, weavers, and a shoemaker. The ministers of the Secession Churches were educated men but they were largely drawn from the same class as their congregations and this common background probably contributed much to the success of their cause. Yet even Seceders were not immune to the new ideas taking over in religious matters. Many had come, by the later years of the century, to believe that changes in doctrine and worship might be made, after careful and mature consideration, in the light of new circumstances. Opposing them dissenting groups, who held that the 17th century Covenants had laid down the tenets of Presbyterianism for all time and were immutable, broke away from the Burghers in 1799, and from the Anti-Burghers in 1806, to set up their own separate Churches known as the "Auld Lichts". The original secession had fragmentised into four bodies although the Auld Lichts of both Burghers and Anti-Burghers were to exist only briefly. In Largs the New Licht principles seem to have been accepted without controversy, or at least without open schism.

Within the Established Church patronage continued to cause disputes which led to a second secession. In 1761 the Rev. Thomas Gillespie, minister of Carnock, and a few like-minded followers constituted a Presbytery "of Relief for Christians oppressed in their Church Privileges". The Relief Church differed from the Churches of the earlier secession by being much more liberal. It saw itself not as antagonistic but as complementary to the Established Church, from which it differed in severing itself from state control by reserving the congregational right to select ministers. As in the case of the original secession, it was to be many years before a Relief congregation was formed in Largs.

Over the years change came gradually but unmistakably in the established Church. Services became shorter, though still long by modern standards; the Holy Fairs gave place to regular but still infrequent celebrations of Communion in each individual church; the dispensation of the Sacrament continued to be regarded with the greatest reverence but tent preachings were reduced until they disappeared altogether; ministers and elders no longer felt it necessary to visit parishioners in order to catechise them and enquire into their religious observances within the family; and discipline cases before the Kirk Session, though by no means abandoned, became less frequent. Secession ministers criticised their parish colleagues, accusing them of concentrating on secular interests such as literature or farming, and of cultivating connections with the upper classes to the neglect of less privileged parishioners whom it was their duty to serve.

That there was some basis to the charges was proved when the Rev. Dr Thomas Chalmers, one of the outstanding Church leaders of the early 19th century, as a young man published a pamphlet in which he argued that a minister could satisfactorily discharge all his parochial duties in two days each week leaving the other five "for the prosecution of any science in which his taste may dispose him to engage". In later years, when he was prominent in an Evangelical revival within the Church, Chalmers openly admitted the error of this view but it was no more than an extreme example of the "Moderate" views prevalent in the late 18th century Church. Of course, many ministers faithfully served all their parishioners and in an isolated country charge like Largs new ideas would be slow to gain acceptance. Even so, the local population cannot have been entirely oblivious to the permissiveness that was infiltrating the Church. So little is known of Stephen Rowan that it is impossible to assess his reaction to changing conditions or to evaluate how he carried out his parochial duties. Certainly, his Church was not in the forefront of progress. Some twenty years previously, Sunday Schools had been set up to give the children of the very poor basic instruction, chiefly, though not entirely, religious. In some quarters it was suspected that these could be used to inculcate false doctrine or, worse still, radical ideas. The Largs Kirk Session was cautious. It even went to the extent of paying out 3s 6d in expenses to seven persons, "teachers in Sunday Schools", to appear before it. Their testimony cannot have been impressive for the Session decided to have no truck with the innovation and it was to be ten years before a Sunday School was set up.

Other disbursements of the Session show a variety of charitable outlays. In 1795 John Crawford of Fairlie received £1 "to assist him to by a cow"; in March 1800, 3s 6d was spent on the rather mysterious purpose of sending "a swindler" to Mr Hunter of Hunterstown; and later in the same year John Beith from "the Back of the World" was given 2s and cloth to have a coat made.

About 1798 the Session undertook to pay the costs of bringing up "a foundling child", though by 1800 it would appear that the poor little waif had died. The first mention of a donation to the Royal Infirmary of Glasgow was made in 1800; it being apparently understood that, in return, patients from Largs would be admitted to that institution. The subscription list had 30 signatures and raised £24 in sums ranging from 5s to 3 guineas. Stephen Rowan himself contributed 3 guineas, and when it was proposed to acquire a hearse "for the decent conveyance of the dead from the more distant parts of this large parish" he gave £5, though no one else on the list gave more than £1.

Among the office-bearers, John Dun, the schoolmaster, was appointed Session Clerk in 1791. He was followed in both positions by John McLean, who held the post of clerk only until 1800 when the new schoolmaster, Gilbert Graham, was appointed.

In 1801 "Bailie" Greg, because of "advancing years and increasing infirmities", resigned from the post of Kirk Treasurer and was succeeded by John Beith – presumably not the same John Beith who had the previous year been without a coat to his back. In 1798 William Shearer, the bellman, gave place to William Jamieson, the first of three generations to hold that post. Stephen Rowan died on 4th June, 1801. His widow went to Ayr where she died on 15th January, 1815 at the age of 70.

JOHN MITCHELL

The 19th century brought sweeping changes and a minister of some distinction. John Mitchell was born in Cupar, Fife, in 1772. After qualifying in theology at Edinburgh University he was licensed by the Presbytery of Greenock on 17th December 1793, but continued his studies. In 1801 he received the degree of Doctor of Medicine for a thesis *"De Phthisi Pulmonali"* from the University of Edinburgh. He was presented as minister to Largs Church by Hugh, Earl of Eglinton in November 1801; and ordained and inducted on 22nd April, 1802. On 5th September 1803, he married Mary Carstairs.

At this time the seaside had become fashionable and Largs shared in its popularity. Men who had acquired modest fortunes abroad, retired to Largs, and rich merchants from Glasgow and Paisley and Greenock built "marine villas" where they and their families spent much of the year. They employed indoor servants, grooms, gardeners, and crews for the yachts – which for many of them were an integral part of their life in Largs. Most of the newcomers took an active interest in local affairs and they brought a wider perspective of the world to what had been a remote little town.

In 1820, George Robertson published a *Topographical Description of Ayrshire*. Comparison of his survey of the Parish of Largs with that given in Sinclair's *Statistical Account* shows how the place had been transformed in only two decades. The resident population had doubled from an estimated 1,025 in 1796, to 2,272 in 1818 – of whom 800 lived in the town itself. Weavers, numbering 180, formed the major part of the working people:

> "Most of these are employed by the Manufacturers of Paisley, in various branches of the Muslin or Silk fabrics; while the remainder are employed in the more steady customary work of weaving linen or other stuffs for the thrifty country good-wives; which if it does not afford them so high wages sometimes as the first, neither does it leave them altogether idle at any time."

A map drawn in 1811 shows the land south of the Gogo between the Broomfields and the road laid out in sites as "The New Town of Largs". The grandiose scheme never properly materialised for the firstcomers took not one but several feus, so that the attractive Georgian layout was spoilt and the remaining sites would have overlooked kitchen gardens and outhouses. Robertson described them and named the first owners:

> "In the vicinity of Largs, there has been of late a considerable extent of ground taken off, by different persons, in feu from the estate of Brisbane, in parcels more or less from half an acre each, up to 2, 3, or 4; and in one case to the extent of 8 acres. On all these, there has been set down some remarkably elegant villas, in the finest taste, each amid its own gardens and shrubbery. The view, from them all, abounds in that greatly-diversified scenery, which the Firth of Clyde here exhibits, in various combinations, with the coast of Cowal and the different islands of Bute, Arran and the Cumbraes. The different proprietors of these are the following:
>
> | | |
> |---|---|
> | Mrs Boyd | Robert Lang Esq |
> | Dr Francis Brown | Rev.John Leech |
> | John Carnie Esq. | Thomas Maxwell Esq. |
> | John Ewing Esq. | Rev.Dr Mitchell |
> | J Jamieson Esq. | Hugh Morris Esq. |
> | James Long Esq. | Mrs Wyllie |
>
> There is also a handsome villa, almost within the town, belonging to Captain Robert Morrice; called Muirburn House; and at a little distance in the same quarter stands the Manse, a house of some shew".

The growth of Largs was due, at least in part, to easier transport. Roads had vastly improved as Robertson commented:

> "An excellent turnpike road traverses the whole length of the parish by the shore side, affording ready access to Greenock on the one hand, and Ardrossan, Saltcoats, Irvine &c on the other; besides being of vast benefit to the internal communication of one part of the parish with another. There has, not many years ago, been a very good turnpike road made across the parish, to the eastward of Largs, by the vale of Kelburn, towards Dalry and Kilbirnie; and there is another in forwardness up the vale of Brisbane, towards Greenock and Port Glasgow, which, when completed, will render the communication to this parish, from other parts, among the most accommodating in the County."

A regular stage-coach service between Ayr and Greenock ran through Largs three times a week and, for those who preferred to travel privately, there were post-chaises for hire.

In 1812 the Comet sailed on the Clyde. Die-hard skippers snorted that they preferred the winds of heaven to the devil's fire and brimstone, but the future lay with the steamship. It opened up the Firth, turning small seaports and fishing villages into holiday resorts. Not that the invention was accepted without reservations. In *The Ayrshire Legatees* John Galt described how the Rev. Zachariah Pringle and his family set out from the imaginary parish of "Garnock" for London to claim a fortune they had inherited. They travelled from Irvine to Greenock by coach, changing horses at Largs – no doubt at the main posting inn, the Brisbane Arms, now the George Hotel. The journey from Greenock to Glasgow was made by steamboat in spite of Dr Pringle's "misgivings about the engine". But, setting aside his "concern for the boiler", he found it "surprising comfortable" being provided with "a good fire in a carron grate in the middle of the floor and books to read". The Pringles crossed from Glasgow to Edinburgh by coach and sailed from Leith to London. From there in a letter to his Session Clerk, the Rev. Zachariah sent instructions that his congregation in Garnock must not fail to return thanks on the following Sunday for the family's safe arrival. Travelling was still not to be lightly undertaken!

Yet enthusiastic visitors to Largs could regard the hazards of the journey as part of the adventure of their holiday. Robertson wrote:

"Though it is not of very long standing that Largs has been celebrated for sea-bathing, yet the general purity of the air, conjoined with the facility with which bathing can, at all times of the tide, be accomplished, seems now to have established its fame. The ready conveyance betwixt the populous city of Glasgow and this place, by means of the steam-boats, must have a tendency also, to increase the number of visitors. The country too, through which these pass, abounds with the finest scenery imaginable. The very sail itself, must be exhilarating to valetudinary people; whilst the voyage may admit of their friends paying them a visit, every day if they chuse. The distance by water from Glasgow is about 38 miles; the voyage is performed in about 5 hours; the cabin fare is only 5s 6d."

Seeing this new opportunity opening up before them, the Largs people wasted no time in exploiting it. A good deal of work went into improving the houses in the town to make them more attractive to visitors. Robertson noted that there were "two good Inns in the village" and added that new houses

"built on speculation for bathing quarters, among which Mr T Underwood's and Mr Cochrane's may be stated as specimens of genteel and commodious lodgings".

Even the minister took advantage of the new market. John Mitchell built a "cottage" on the Broomfields and it was his practice to let either it or the Manse to summer visitors.

Provisions had also to be made for the entertainment of the holiday makers.

> "The increasing influx of strangers for sea-bathing, and of whom many are in a genteel line of life, occasioned Baths, on an elegant plan, to be built for their accommodation. These are constructed either for warm or cold bathing, as may be required. They were erected by subscription, and opened for the public in June 1816. One end of the building consists of a public room, 44 feet by 24, for assemblies, and in the bathing season, is used as a reading room, to which strangers are admitted by the season, month, or week, as it may suit them."

By 1825, a commercial directory could write that Largs had:

> "a greater number of visitors during the season than any other watering place in the county. The very superior style of the lodging-houses entitles it to the very extensive patronage bestowed upon it"

and it was promised that "a company of comedians" would attend during the season for the further amusement of visitors.

Events followed much the same course in Fairlie. Some of the more substantial houses were taken over by town dwellers and modernised as holiday homes, and villas "in a very uncommon style of elegance" were built on ground feued in 1816.

> "Fairley is also used as a bathing station, but it is not so well adapted to the purpose as Largs. The time of bathing must be limited to the water when it is full in-shore; as it retires fast back on the ebb of tide to a great distance."

Across the county border in Renfrewshire, plans were drawn up for Wemyss Bay. Again, the elaborate project resulted only in a few houses. South of the Kelly Burn, within the Parish of Largs, there was a little expansion but the real development of Skelmorlie did not take place until the middle of the century.

The swiftly changing life of Largs exercised a profound effect on the years of John Mitchell's ministry. The increase in both permanent and temporary residents "in a genteel line of life" presented problems for the Parish Church. Obviously the ancient church was no longer adequate to fulfil its functions, and, less able than the later Skelmorlie Aisle to withstand time, it had fallen into disrepair. Two sites were available for its successor: one in School Street and the other at the end of Gallowgate. Fortunately, after much discussion, the latter was chosen and the building of a new church was begun.

The memorial stone was laid amongst scenes of general rejoicing, the day being declared a public holiday and the tradesmen parading the streets headed by a band. In a cavity of the stone were placed coins of George II and George III, a copy of the *"Greenock Advertiser and Clyde and West Country Chronicle"* dated 15th May 1811, and a statement which read:

> "The foundation-stone of the Church was laid in the fifty-fifth year of the reign of His Majesty George the Third in the seventy-fourth year of his age and in the year of our Lord one thousand eight hundred and eleven this sixteenth day of May by Colonel Thomas Brisbane of Brisbane Provincial Grand Master of the Shire of Air under the Grand Lodge of Scotland."

The heritors paid two thirds of the cost. The remainder was raised from members of the congregation, who were to receive "sittings" in proportion to their contributions, and it was recorded that the allocation of pews was settled "amicably". The contractor was Robert Napier and the building was in a style sometimes scoffingly termed "Heritors' Gothic". Yet the heritors' concern for their pockets often resulted in a simplicity that was in good taste and not unattractive.

The new church was rectangular, with pointed Gothic windows, and was surmounted by a tower. The external appearance is clearly shown in Swan's picture of Largs in the 1820s. Because funds were short, the steeple was reduced by ten feet from the original plan, but it had what Robertson described as "an excellent clock" with a painted face. The clock was undoubtedly an ornament to the town and of the greatest utility to the inhabitants, but it did prove later to be a drain on Church resources. There were frequent small payments to William Jamieson for "minding the clock" and cleaning it, while in 1822, John Hill and Henry Duncan had to be called in and paid £2. 15s for repairing it.

Inside the church was accommodation for over 900 worshippers. A large single gallery, supported by turned wooden pillars, ran round the north, west and south walls. The pulpit, with raised stairs at either side, was originally set against the east gable, though latterly it stood well out from the wall. In front of the pulpit was the Precentor's box, in which ten successive "Uptakkers of the Psalm" were to serve. At those Baptisms which took place in church, fathers brought their children up the south pulpit stair and presented them before a simple bowl extended from the pulpit wall, on which there was also hung a towel.

A new bell, inscribed "T. MEARNS. LONDON. FECIT. 1812. PEACE AND NEIGHBOURHOOD" was mounted in the belfry and for many years rang the congregation to worship. The massive bell was brought to Largs in the Millport sloop owned by William Kerr, and since there was no pier, was landed at the mouth of the Gogo burn in 1814. The fine bell from the demolished church seems to have gone to Port Glasgow where some misguided person painted it and spoiled its tone. It was then suggested that the defect might be remedied by having it boiled! The result does not seem to have been recorded and the bell ultimately found its way to the West Indies.

There are accounts of celebrations at various stages in the erection of the new church, but little seems to have survived regarding its dedication. When it came into use in 1812, it was generally regarded as a great advance and it did have a title to fame, which was not then apparent and is now often forgotten. It was the Church in which John Dunmore Lang, the son of a local farmer, must have worshipped as a boy. He left Largs to study for the ministry at the University of Glasgow, and after his ordination by the Presbytery of Irvine on 30th September 1822, he emigrated to Australia to become the founder of the Presbyterian Church there, and a statesman of some note. The simple little Largs Church can be said to have been the mother church of Presbyterianism in Australia.

The old church was sold to Mr Hill, a local mason. Soon afterwards, a small crowd gathered in the graveyard to see the funeral of a member of the crew of *HMS Shearwater* which was stationed at Largs on the Clyde survey. Boys climbing on the derelict church dislodged some of the stones. One was killed and the accident hastened the demolition of the building. As a burial place, the

Skelmorlie Aisle was left intact, and a fragment of wall to which was affixed a Boyle Family memorial – now much eroded – was also preserved. Stones from the old church were said to have been used to build the wall round the graveyard, and the ground on which the church actually stood was subsequently used for burials.

In all the flurry and excitement of a growing town and a new church, the routine of the congregation continued. John Mitchell was something of a disciplinarian, for, on more than one occasion, he refused to baptise children whose parents did not regularly attend public worship until the parents had mended their ways. In 1806 the Session decided that they would prefer "one of our own number" as Clerk in place of Gilbert Graham who was not an elder. They appointed John Beith to take over the Clerk's duty in addition to those he already held as Treasurer. On 21st June 1822, there is a note: "Pd the young man that priched that day £1. 10s" and this would seem to be the first record of how much the Church paid for pulpit supply. Already in 1824 doubts were being expressed that the new church was too small, and there was some internal re-arrangement of doors and passages to provide a little extra accommodation. In 1825 there is an odd entry: "Payd John Arthor for the time Mr Mitchell was in his hous". John Arthur was the owner of the White Hart Inn and it can only be surmised that some domestic disaster in the Manse had forced the Session to board out the minister while repairs were effected. The lack of friction between the two Largs congregations was proved in October 1825, when the Burghers were given permission to use the Parish Church while their own meeting-house was being rebuilt.

The Church had also to continue its oversight of education. About 1809, the heritors built a school with a house for the schoolmaster above it. Robertson reported that there were in the Parish School, under the charge of Gilbert Graham, between 60 and 90 pupils, the number being greater in winter than in summer, and the curriculum had been extended to include elocution, book-keeping, English grammar, and the first principles of Greek. A private school run by Mr Hall, and another by Mr Beith, had a combined roll rather greater than that of the parish school. Small schools at Fairlie, Skelmorlie, and Whittlieburn received a small amount of financial assistance from the Church. The school at Whittlieburn was intended for children too young to make the daily journey to Largs and a similar school was set up at the Meigle by a one-armed Waterloo veteran named Quintin Logan.

Largs had developed as a playground for those with money, and as a source of prosperity for local people who could supply their needs. But underneath, there was another Largs that was the immediate concern of the church. Robertson wrote in 1820:

> "the number of poor, permanent on the roll, is 32, and occasionally relieved 15 or 20. There is distributed among them, annually, about £150."

These were only routine pensions paid to parishioners too old or infirm to support themselves. The Church had more extensive social responsibilities.

By the 19th century, records are less sparse and they show that the poor looked to the Church for help in a wide variety of emergencies. That vagrants were still dealt with in summary fashion as shown by the entry:

> "a poor woman that was brought from Kilbrid to us and wee sant her to Grinock."

Spelling was very much a matter of personal taste, and the keeper of the Session accounts produced some pleasing variants:

> "to a poor sailor in needsisity"
> "to a poor man that was shipraced"
> "to a poor woman and child from Greenock Infirmity"
> "to a poor seaman that was shiprect belonging to Americy"

Repercussions of the Napoleonic wars are seen in several payments to soldiers' wives and widows, who seem to have regarded Largs as a staging post on the way home to Ireland.

Travelling people showed an unfortunate tendency to be taken ill within the bounds of the Parish:

> "to a poor woman that was not weel from Johnston Bridge"
> "payd a poor woman with 3 children ill of the messle"

The sums distributed were small, usually about 1s; but 5s can hardly be considered an over-generous response to the predicament of

> "a poor man on his way home to Mushlburh who had his wife delivered of two children at Fairlie".

Not that local people were overlooked. The family of James Cochrane received "a boll of meal"; the Widow McLen was given two yards of "pleden" to mend her blankets and later a sum of money for "cordials"; Hugh Gouldy in Fairlie had £1 to mend his cart; John Boyd was paid £1. 18s for "rent due to him by Isbela Duncan" and there are several notes of poor children being given shoes or clothing. The list is long and surprisingly varied. The work of the Church was not only spiritual; it was also extremely practical. The individual items were trivial but they must have been of immense value to the recipients and the total outlay was not inconsiderable when church door collections rarely amounted to much more than £1 each Sunday.

There are quite a few references to payments towards buying coffins. For the poor, even a modest burial could be difficult; for those with greater resources, funeral expenses could be substantial, as is shown by two surviving accounts.

"Acc of My Mothers funeral who Departed this Life upon Sunday morning at 5 of the clock, 13 March Anno 1796, Interred 15th Inst. upon Tuesday at 3 o'clock noon.

To 5 half galls Rum @ 12s gall	3.	3.	0
To 10 galls Wine, Reid & White, @ 10s per gall	5.	0.	0
To 5 pecks Short Bread @ 5s 6d per peck	1.	7.	6
To 12 lbs Shuggar Biscuit @ 1s 7d per lb		19.	0
To Warning Grave and Bell		5.	0
To Mortcloth		6.	0
To Covering the Hand Spokes			4
To John Lochead for carriage of the spirits		6.	0
To the Coffen	1	5.	0

In addition there was 7s for "a Head Stone Bought at Stevenstown" and £1. 11s for working and lettering it. The other account shows different priorities:

"My Father Departed this Life 15th April 1811.
Funeral Expenses and Sundries:

To Coffin to John Boyd	1.	16.	0
To Mortcloth Bell and Warning To W Jamieson		12.	0
To Bread from Charles McArthur	2.	11.	6
To Alexander Bruce to Sundreys	6.	1.	0
To Sundry Expences		2.	0
To Agnes M. a gown		14.	0

To Jean F.	1.	0
To Janet & Margaret T.	15.	0
To Janet T.	5.	0

But a new and active Church and a growing congregation were not enough to satisfy John Mitchell. He demitted the charge on his appointment to the Chair of Divinity at St Mary's College, St Andrews, on 16th May 1826. He received the honorary degree of Doctor of Divinity at St Andrews on 20th January 1827, and died on 14th November, 1835. Mary Carstairs died on 9th November, 1874.

JACOB RICHARDSON

Immediately after John Mitchell's departure the heritors requested that a Mr Robert Crawford should supply at a salary of 27s 6d per Sunday. But the vacancy was soon filled. Jacob Richardson was born in Dumfriesshire and educated at the University of Edinburgh. He was tutor in the family of Mr Charteris of Amisfield but, licensed by the Presbytery of Dumfries on 6th November 1810, he became assistant to the Rev. Alexander Scott DD, Minister of Dumfries. Richardson was presented to Largs Church by the trustees of Archibald, Earl of Eglinton, and ordained there on 26th September,1826. He married Wilhemina, the only daughter of Dr Scott, on 25th November 1826. Jacob Richardson was said to be a man of warm heart and dignified presence but his ministry was to be short and tragic. Such records as exist imply that under him the Church continued its usual course. Thus in January 1828, "three salars that was rect near Danmark" were given 1s; and in February, 3s was spent on "a Bible for a child". Other routine charitable donations were made though one may suspect something slightly bogus about:

"John Foster a ministers son that was taken by a paryt [presumably pirate] and med his escape travelling from Grenock to Air".

In 1828 a serious outbreak of dysentery raised the death rate in Largs as it did in much of the west of Scotland. In 1826, the suggestion that a new Manse should be built was rejected but repairs carried out in the following year give some indication of the domestic arrangements in the Manse and in similar houses. The glebe walls were restored; the well and washing houses were repaired and "a new necessary house" was built.

There appeared to be nothing untoward in the life of the Church until 6th October 1830, when Jacob Richardson shot himself. It was recalled that the last sermon he preached was on the theme "One shall plant but another shall reap" so that the thought of suicide was perhaps already on his mind. *Fraser's Magazine,* a popular periodical of the time, printed a note that was generally supposed to refer to Jacob Richardson:

> "A clergyman in the Church of Scotland loved one woman, married another, having been enslaved for the moment by the passion for gold. The furies of remorse immediately assailed him, and they came from without – the furies of Scottish wrath at his mean and mercenary deed. He was a proud and sensitive man and one Sunday morning, not having the courage to face his congregation, he shot himself. Oh, my friends! I do not say let us be very pitiful for this is easy; let us be very merciful, for this is difficult".

Whether this rather fanciful tale of an unhappy love affair was in fact the reason for the fit of depression in which Jacob Richardson took his own life may be doubted. What is without doubt, is that the event left the Church and the town in a state of shock.

Wilhelmina Richardson feued a piece of ground in the north Kirklands and built the house named Rosebank. She played an active part in the Ladies' Committee that supervised the Female School of Industry until her death on 3rd February, 1855.

JOHN DOW

Born in Dunkeld in 1788, John Dow was educated at the University of Edinburgh and was for some time a teacher in George Watson's School. He later became tutor in the family of Sir James Montgomery Cuningham of Corsehill and was licensed by the Presbytery of Irvine on 24th November, 1818. He was presented by the trustees of Archibald, Earl of Eglinton, and ordained in Largs Church on 28th April, 1831.

The first three decades of the 19th century had brought change to the town of Largs. The fourth and fifth were to bring even greater change to the Church, both locally and nationally. It is now quite difficult to appreciate how extensive interest was in the affairs of the Church at that time. Throughout the whole century, religious leaders were as well-known and as newsworthy as the political figures of today. By extending the franchise, the Reform Act of 1832 gave more people a say in secular government and many came to believe that a similar freedom should apply with regard to the Church.

For many years the Scottish Church had regularly, as a matter of routine, appealed to Parliament to rescind the Patronage Act; with the same regularity, as a matter of routine, Westminster rejected the plea. Seceders resented having to pay a tax, based on the old teinds, which went in some part to the maintenance of the Established church. Discussion of these points became widespread as the rationalist and nationalist climate that had underlain political reform was applied to religious questions.

A substantial body of opinion concluded that the Church should be disestablished and supported only by voluntary contributions. Opposed to these "Voluntaries" was the belief that the Presbyterian system of Church government, by setting up its own courts, presented a threat to the State that could only be avoided by legislative control. The problems at issue were not simply a splitting of theological hairs. They were of fundamental concern to the whole place of the Church in the modern State and to its relationship with society in general. Nor was this limited only to Scotland. Similar difficulties arose in other European countries where the Reformation had produced Calvinist Churches.

However, the early events of John Dow's ministry were hardly controversial. He was remembered in Largs with some affection. It was his practice when visiting outlying parts of the Parish, or going to Greenock, to walk barefoot across the moor. He carried his stockings and shoes slung on a stick over his shoulder and stopped to put them on only when he was within sight of his destination. On one occasion when preaching, he was so aroused by the thought of Jonah being swallowed by the whale, that his gesticulations swept his notes out of the pulpit. For a moment he surveyed the papers on the floor, and then he observed, "and Jonah – like me – found

Largs Parish Church built in 1812 and showing the transepts added in 1832.

himself in a novel and awkward predicament". It was said that Dow could visit even the poorest of his parishioners on terms of friendship and equality. He held three services each Sunday, and he himself led the praise at the evening service to allow his precentor, William Shedden, to remain at home looking after the children while his wife attended church.

The Poor Relief fund had to deal with an outbreak of cholera in 1832, but otherwise continued its customary work. The entry:

"Paid Agnes Banantine by order of Session six days for
working hay at Fichen for Mary and Margaret Crawford 7/-"

suggests help for two women working a farm on their own; and the ability to deal promptly with sudden emergency is shown by:

"For lodging 3 children got on the street on Saterday night
til Mondy 2/3d"

As a former schoolmaster, John Dow inspected the Parish School in great detail; and difficulty arose with regard to Gilbert Graham.

He had apparently been licensed as a minister, and occasionally preached quite acceptably in Largs Church; but he had become elderly and it was felt that he should hand over his duties as parish schoolmaster to a younger man. Graham did not object. He asked only for a "character" to assist him in finding alternative employment. Seeing this as the solution to their problem, the Kirk Session composed a testimonial in glowing terms, and thus scored a quite outstanding own goal. Thereafter, whenever the question of retirement was raised, Graham produced the document as proof positive of his competence. It was not until 1841 that he was succeeded by Alexander Jack. Pigot's Directory for 1825 added a new scholastic establishment in the town. Jane Young is described as dealing in tea and running a boarding academy for young ladies.

With the growth and popularity of Largs, the makeshift arrangements for unloading freight at the mouth of the Gogo proved quite inadequate. Passengers embarking or disembarking had to be rowed out to the steamships in small boats, and after "two most lamentable accidents" in which eight people were drowned, it was decided that the construction of a pier and a harbour was essential. Sir Thomas Brisbane gave the ground in return for shares in the company, and an Act of Parliament was secured in May,1832. The foundation stone was laid with masonic honours on 10th January 1833, although the work was by then already in progress, and the pier came into use on 1st December, 1834. The cost was £4,275 held in 50 lots by 31 shareholders. Very soon the pier was not only bringing in 6% dividend, but also adding to the number of visitors in Largs.

On 1st March 1832, within a year of his arrival in Largs, John Dow called a meeting of the heritors
> "to Consider the existing necessity of providing accommodation in the Parish Church for the numerous parishioners who, on account of the smallness of the present church, are entirely excluded from the same."

Quite apart from the obvious pressure on space during the summer season, Dow presented elaborate statistics to prove that the church could not even provide for the resident population.
> "Those present having taken into consideration the statement of Mr Dow, were unanimously of opinion that there was a want of church accommodation,

and that the church should be enlarged and the meeting should be adjourned till...sketches of plans of the best method of effecting the addition would be ready for laying before the heritors for their consideration, information and guidance. The Rev. Mr Dow was requested to intimate the adjourned meeting to the non-resident heritors."

After preliminary work on the proposal, a further meeting was held on 1st June 1832, when there were present:

"The Right Hon The Earl of Glasgow; Messrs: Robert Wallace of Kelly, Commissioner for General Sir Thos Brisbane; Robert Sinclair for himself; John Scott, Hawkhill; and Christopher Scott of Blackhouse; Wm Lang, Burnside; John Beith, Ladeside; James Wilson, Haylie; John Hair, East Grassyards; Robert Morris, Muirburn; Robert Lang, Blacksorrow; Dr Lang; John Beith for Jas Greg of Middleton; and – Jamieson, Craigton; Bailie Greg, Constablewood."

The Earl of Glasgow was chosen as preses, and four plans for the proposed addition were laid before the meeting showing how some 410 sittings could be gained at an estimated expense of about £525.

"The meeting having taken into mature consideration the best modes for defraying the expense of this enlargement, came to the unanimous opinion that the heritors ought to borrow such a sum from the fund belonging to the poor as would be requisite to effect this enlargement, and that they ought to pay five per cent therefor, which interest will be raised from the rents of the new sittings; and that whatever additional revenue may be realised from these rents shall be accumulated as a sinking fund to repay the principal borrowed. It being distinctly understood that whenever the whole sum is paid up, that the addition to the church shall remain as the property of the heritors, and the rent realised therefrom devoted to such purposes as they may think proper."

A committee was appointed to oversee the work.

"The Earl of Glasgow or his factor; Sir Thomas Brisbane or his commissioner or factor; The Earl of Eglinton or his factor; Mr Wilson, Haylie; Mr Sinclair for the Messrs Scott; Mr William Lang, Burnside or Dr Lang; Capt Morris, Muirburn; Bailie Greg and the Rev. Mr Dow – the last to be convener."

Four tenders for the work were considered on 23rd June, 1832.

"1st: Mr John Paterson still adheres to his former offer for completing the whole work of £523; 2nd: Alexander Carsewell's estimate for the same is £525; 3rd: David Sands estimate is £460; and 4th: Wm McCall's is £457. The committee, having naturally considered these offers, and the characters of the tradesmen, are unanimously of opinion that the work should be let to Mr Wm McCall at his offer of £457."

In the event, after some alterations to the original scheme, the total cost was £593. Of this sum, ten guineas went to Mr John Paterson, builder, for drawing up the plan for the extension which consisted of adding transepts at the east end, thus transforming the church into a cruciform ground plan.

At the same time, the overcrowding in Largs Church was further reduced as a result of the connection of Dr Thomas Chalmers with the Parish. Chalmers was one of the leaders of an evangelical movement which aimed to revitalize the Scottish Church. He believed that the old parish system had adequately served the rural past but that in the new conditions produced by the Industrial Revolution, social chaos could only be averted if spiritual values were predominant and if the upper and middle classes dedicated themselves to the service of the community as benefactors and leaders. Industrialisation had led to a vast shifting of population so that there were no longer churches in the areas where people lived. Chalmers was instrumental in a programme of building new churches chiefly, though not solely, in the overcrowded towns. He himself left the Tron Church in Glasgow to become minister of the new parish of St John's, where many of his fashionable congregation from the Tron associated themselves with the work he undertook there in religious education and social welfare.

Among those inspired by the ideas of social responsibility that Chalmers preached, were two wealthy Glasgow merchants: Charles Stuart Parker, whose family business traded with the West Indies from Glasgow and Liverpool; and Hugh Tennent of Wellpark Breweries. They had holiday homes in Fairlie and, at their own expense, built a school in the village with a dwelling house attached for the village schoolmaster.

Chalmers was a personal friend of both, and after he became Professor of Divinity at the University of Edinburgh in 1828, he visited Fairlie from time to time, especially as the guest of the Parker family. It was almost certainly as a result of his interest and encouragement that the erection of a Chapel of Ease in the village was begun by public subscription. Chapels of Ease were small churches intended to make it easier for people, in outlying parts of a parish, to attend public worship regularly. They had their own ministers who were, in reality, little more than assistants to the parish ministers; and both they and their elders were members of the Kirk Session of the parent church without representation in the Presbytery. The Chapel of Ease in Fairlie – now the nave of the present church – was dedicated on 13th April 1834, and, though the actual date is uncertain, the Rev. James Gardner was appointed "preacher of the Gospel". In a letter to Charles Stuart Parker dated 19th July 1834, Thomas Chalmers wrote:

> "I am to write to Mr Dow. I take the greatest interest in his parochial operations. What has been done for Fairley is quite beautiful and will tell, I think, most beneficially in the way of an example. I hope you continue to have great comfort in the services of your new church."

Another change took place in 1834. For many years the Synod of Argyll had advocated the setting up of a Presbytery in Greenock, as this would be a more convenient meeting place for the representatives of many of its southern parishes. The proposal was adopted and, in spite of some protest from the Presbytery of Irvine, the Parishes of Largs and the Cumbraes were transferred to the new Presbytery of Greenock.

The Evangelical Party had a majority in the General Assembly of 1834. In their enthusiasm for church reform, they passed two measures which were to have weighty consequences and to initiate the Ten Years' Conflict that led up to the Disruption. These were the Veto Act and the Chapels Act. The Scottish Church had contrived to live with lay patronage by making strenuous efforts to ensure that there was congregational assent to the appointment of the patron's nominee, or at least the appearance of assent. The Veto Act was intended to give this policy legal sanction by laying down that a proposed minister would be rejected if a majority of the heads of households in full membership of the church objected to his appointment. The Act was bound to lead to trouble. Patrons naturally resented the curtailment of their privileges and since the heads of households in their wisdom were required only to declare that they were motivated by conscientious regard for the spiritual interests of the congregation, there was virtually no safeguard against frivolous or malicious objections.

The Chapels Act was equally contentious. In order to promote the movement for church extension, it was decided that new churches should be given full status by the creation of *quoad sacra* parishes. Under this, the original civil parish would remain intact, but a part of it could be detached and assigned to a new church in order to give it independence, and its minister full membership of the church courts. But not everyone shared the passion for church extension. The parish church remained responsible for social welfare, financed largely from church door collections. These had already been reduced by the adherence of so many people to the seceding congregations. The creation of new parishes meant a further diversion of funds, thus increasing the burden on the heritors.

Almost immediately, disputes arose and became increasingly acrimonious. Test cases began to drag their ponderous way through the civil courts. Eventually a bemused House of Lords ruled that parishioners' objections had no standing against the rights of patrons and that the redefinition of parish boundaries lay outwith the jurisdiction of the Church. To many people, these two judgements were intolerable State interference in matters that were the sole concern of the Church. In the face of wide-ranging discontent, the Largs Kirk Session met on 12th April 1840, and taking into consideration

> "that the Presbytery of Greenock at their last meeting on the 1st of this month, and in obedience to a recommendation of the Commission of the General Assembly, had resolved that the several congregations within their bounds should be invited to meet on Thursday, 30th of this month for devotional exercises on account of the present critical position of the Church...".

The Kirk Session approved of the matter and unanimously resolved that there should be public worship in the Church of Largs on the 30th day of April at half past 2 o'clock pm. and a prayer meeting in the evening of the same day, both in reference to this important subject. But prayer and meditation could make little headway against positions that were by that time deeply entrenched.

John Dow was perhaps relieved at this juncture to turn his attention to a less controversial matter. It had been decided to issue a *New Statistical Account of Scotland* recording the changes of the last fifty years. Once again parish ministers were called upon to compile it; but though it was more "statistical" than its predecessor, it lacked the personal approach that had pervaded the original. However, John Dow took his responsibilities seriously. His account of the history both of the town and Church show that he had made some study of the subject, and where he felt himself incompetent to discuss any subject, he obtained – and acknowledged – the help of collaborators. Dr John Campbell, a highly esteemed medical practitioner in Largs, whose Memorial Fountain still stands on Mackerston Green, though it has not played for years, contributed the section on Public Health. Geology was dealt with by William Montgomery; Parochial Economy and Industry by James Wilson of Haylie; and Conchology, Botany, and Zoology by the Rev. David Landsborough of Stevenston, an acknowledged expert in the field, who paid compliment to the comprehensive and scientifically arranged collection of sea shells made by the Misses Muir of Warriston.

To Dow's enumeration of landowners, rentals, and tradesmen is added information about church membership which makes it possible to compile a record of the religious affiliations of the Parish. In Fairlie there were 450 people. In 1820 the New Lichts of Burgher and Anti-Burgher Churches had united to form the United Secession Church. Since there never had been an Anti-Burgher congregation in Largs, this was a change in name only and in 1842, when Dow wrote, there were 600 people attached to the United Secession Church.

In Webster's enumeration of the population of Scotland in 1755, it was reported that there were no "Papists" in Ayrshire. The Catholic Emancipation Act was passed in 1829, and in 1842 Dow noted that there were 140 Roman Catholics in the Parish of Largs. He added that about 100 people were attached to a new church:

> "A congregation of Relief is now being formed. A small meeting-house has been erected, capable of containing 450 sitters; but hitherto no minister has been ordained."

From these figures Dow calculated that there were left in the Parish 2,214 people who were in membership of the Established

Church or who, having no Church connection, relied upon it for such spiritual assistance as they might require.

The Relief Secession had taken place in 1761 and had made no impact on Largs. However, the Relief Church had been in the forefront of resistance to State intrusion on the Church, and this sudden belated appearance of a congregation may perhaps suggest that Largs had anticipated the future by having its own miniature Disruption in advance of the actual event. For by this time, the possibility of another secession was already being openly discussed. Thomas Chalmers firmly believed that the Church had a responsibility to the State but it was a partnership he envisaged. He was not prepared to accept State domination, and at a meeting in Edinburgh in November 1843, he agreed to resolutions deploring interference by the civil courts in spiritual matters, and, from his experience of church extension, gave it as his opinion that secession was feasible. A nation-wide campaign was initiated to inform Church members of the principles that were believed to be at stake. Public meetings were held and deputations visited country charges in an attempt to prove that the material advantages of establishment must be relinquished in the interest of ecclesiastical independence.

Although he supported the cause of freedom in the Church, John Dow seems to have played a less conspicuous part in the instruction of his congregation than did his assistant Joseph Welsh. Born in 1818, the son of a Greenock merchant, he had graduated Master of Arts at the University of Glasgow in 1837; and, being young and enthusiastic, he spoke frequently and passionately on the need to resist State intrusion before he left Largs to be ordained as minister of Oldham Street Church in Liverpool on 3rd November, 1842. Later, a public meeting was arranged to consider the causes of complaint. However, Captain Morris of Muirburn, a staunch supporter of the Established Church, secured an interdict forbidding the use of the Church for this purpose. The meeting was transferred to the Relief Church; and there some 600 people heard an address by the Rev. Mr McNaught of Paisley.

Feelings ran even higher in Fairlie. Almost immediately after the passing of the Chapels Act in 1834, John Dow presented a petition to the Presbytery of Greenock

> "from a number of individuals residing in or near the village of Fairlie in this parish now attending divine ordinance in a place of worship lately erected there, setting forth the great advantage they had derived from the ministrations of the Preacher stationed among them and craving that he should be ordained and the station erected into a parish."

It was further added that in the village were about 360 persons, with an additional rural population of 100, and that the Church was free of debt and had 300 sittings which were all let. Details were worked out at subsequent meetings and it was agreed that Fairlie should become a *quoad sacra* parish extending from what had been the southern boundary of the Parish of Largs at Fairlie Glen Burn, to the Kel Burn and including

> "both sides of the valley called Rysdale, through which runs the road to Kilburnie."

The Constitution of the new Parish Church laid down that it should be for the exclusive use of the Church of Scotland. The stipend was fixed at £120 to be derived from seat rents and collections, and a sum of £10 annually was to be contributed to the Poor Relief Fund of Largs Church. The Rev. James Gardner was appointed minister and was inducted on 23rd September, 1835. The Rev. James Drummond, minister of Cumbrae, and the Rev. John Dow, minister of Largs

> "appointed by the Presbytery of Greenock for taking the necessary steps to form a Session for the said Parish met with James Gardner on 3rd November 1835, and constituted a Kirk Session of five members from whom the village schoolmaster, James Parlane, formerly an elder in the Largs Church, was elected Clerk".

The Parish of Largs had been divided two centuries after the suggestion had first been made.

The division was to last for only a brief period. James Gardner died on 17th December 1836, after a ministry of eighteen months. He was succeeded by John Gemmel. Born in Port Glasgow in 1807 and educated at Glasgow University, he had served as an assistant to Thomas Chalmers in St John's Parish in Glasgow before becoming minister at Newton Commel in Ireland. He was a conscientious pastor, a scholar of some note – the University of Glasgow subsequently conferred on him the honorary degree of Doctor of Divinity – and he remained an admirer and fervent disciple of his former mentor Thomas Chalmers. When the Chapels Act was declared illegal, the Fairlie Church was demoted once again to the status of a Chapel of Ease wholly dependent on the Parish Church of Largs. The congregation naturally resented the fact that the State had deprived them of the right to rule their own Church. Moreover, the village knew Chalmers well as a frequent visitor and had often

> "been privileged in hearing repeatedly the message of salvation from that eminent man of God."

At one point Chalmers gave a series of talks in the drawing-room of Fairlie House, when forms had to be brought in from the schoolroom to seat a hundred people every evening for a week. Different ministers delivered lectures in the Church on "The Spiritual Freedom of Christ's House" and a Church Defence Association was formed.

A final attempt was made to avert an outcome that was fast becoming inevitable. In March 1843, a Scottish Member of Parliament moved that the House go into committee to consider the grievances of which the Church of Scotland complained. The majority of the Scottish members were in favour, but Westminster as a whole, convinced by this time that the Scottish population were all religious maniacs, decisively defeated the motion. All Scotland waited in excited anticipation of the meeting of the General Assembly on 18th May 1843.

It began in the customary form with the retiring Moderator, Dr David Welsh, preaching the sermon at the opening service in the High Kirk of Edinburgh. But when the Commissioners moved to St Andrews Church, where their meetings were to take place, Welsh rose, not to constitute the Assembly for business, but to intimate that since it was no longer free to make decisions at the dictates of conscience he had no alternative but to withdraw. He bowed to the Queen's representative and left, followed by Chalmers and about one third of the Commissioners, both lay and clerical.

Outside a crowd had gathered. As the numbers who "came out"

increased, the excitement grew more intense. Lord Cockburn, a judge of the Court of Session, described the scene:

> "As soon as Welsh, who wore his Moderator's dress, appeared in the street, and people saw that principle had really triumphed over interest, he and his followers were received with the loudest acclamations. They walked in procession down Hanover Street to Canonmills ... through an unbroken mass of cheering people and beneath innumerable handkerchiefs waving from the windows. But amidst this exultation there was much sadness and many a tear, many a grave face and fearful thought, for no-one could doubt that it was with sore hearts that these ministers left the Church, and no thinking man could look on the unexampled scene and behold that the temple was rent without pain and sad forebodings."

The procession moved to Tanfield Hall. There, joined by ministers and elders from all over the country, they constituted the Free Church of Scotland and held its first General Assembly, electing Chalmers as Moderator. A Deed of Demission was drawn up and signed by the seceding ministers. In it they voluntarily gave up all the payments and privileges they had received in the Established Church. They had then to set themselves to building up, entirely by voluntary contributions, the exact counterpart of the Church they had left. Churches, manses, and stipends were only the most obvious requirements. Provision had to be made for many people who had sacrificed their livelihood and their future by adhering to the Free Church. Training colleges had to be set up to continue the education of divinity students; schoolmasters and private tutors, who had been dismissed, had to be employed; and neither foreign missionaries nor their work could be abandoned. It was a superhuman task undertaken in faith and in the zeal of religious fervour.

As the ripples spread out from Edinburgh, congregations of the Free Church of Scotland were formed all over the country. They met wherever they could: in barns, lofts, store-houses, and, perhaps with some folk memory of the old days of religious persecution, in the open air. At Campbeltown, one congregation was even forced to worship in a distillery. In Largs, John Dow informed a crowded and emotionally affected congregation that as he had signed the Deed of Demission he must immediately leave the Parish Church and Manse. On 10th June 1843, some two hundred former members of the Established Church met in the Brisbane Academy to form a Free

Church congregation in Largs. On 2nd July 1843, Dr Hugh Lang, Dr John Campbell, John Main, Matthew Underwood, and John Cochrane – all formerly elders in the Parish Church – constituted themselves as its Kirk Session. Services were held in the Brisbane Academy in Lade Street, but the congregation soon grew too large to be accommodated there and the Free Church was given permission to meet in the United Secession Church in Waterside Street until their own church was built.

Not a few ministers found that the material sacrifices they made when they signed the Deed of Demission were less painful than the difficulties of carrying on their pastoral work in parishes torn by dissension and broken friendships. John Dow may have been among them. Or, a man already in his fifties, he may have felt that the work of building up a new church required the energy of a younger man. Whatever his reasons, he demitted his charge before the end of July 1843, and it was under his successor, the Rev. David Douie, that plans went ahead to build the Free Church and bring it into use. John Dow was translated to be minister of a very small Free Church congregation at Roberton in the Presbytery of Kelso and Lauder, where he remained until he retired in 1852. He died at Edinburgh in 1865.

In Fairlie, John Gemmel also signed the Deed of Demission. Four of his five elders and the great majority of his congregation joined him in leaving the Established Church. He was cited to appear before the Presbytery at Greenock and, when he failed to do so, his charge was declared vacant by a public intimation in the Parish Church of Largs. The Free Church had believed that it would be able to retain recently built churches and Gemmel continued to preach in the Church which had, after all, been built by local subscription. However, the Presbytery, incensed by the continued use of the Church and by the failure to make the stipulated contribution to the Poor Relief Fund, took legal action in November to repossess the Church. Gemmel moved to the school, which had been built by two members of his congregation. They had obtained permission from the Earl of Glasgow to use the ground, but no formal feu had been granted. Taking advantage of this technicality, the Earl sent his factor and a notary to serve an interdict forbidding the use of the school. The Free Church congregation crossed the road to the stable at Fairlie Lodge and worshipped there throughout the winter. Gemmel was afterwards to say, rather sadly:

"There, exposed to open doors and draughts, I received a severe cold from which I never entirely recovered."

The new Church, a part of which could be partitioned off by folding screens to form a schoolroom, came into use on 31st July, 1844. Almost entirely rebuilt after a disastrous fire in 1879, it is now the Church Hall.

The foundation stone of the Largs Free Church was laid on 28th September 1843, and it was ready for use early in the following year. It was an unpretentious little building and it, too, made provision for a part to be used as a school for classes that had already begun to meet in a room in Gallowgate Square. Shortly before the Disruption actually took place, Sir Thomas Brisbane had presented the Brisbane Academy – now the Stevenson Institute – for the education of the youth of the town. It was passed over to the Free Church and remained under its authority until the State Boards took over responsibility for public education. In 1886 the Free Church was enlarged, reconstructed and ornamented by the addition of an Italianate facade, to become the building which is now St John's Church of Scotland.

The setting up of the Free Church was not the only change in the religious organisation of the Parish of Largs. By a national union in 1847, the United Secession Church and the Relief Church joined together to form the United Presbyterian Church. The recently built Relief Church in Largs was vacated, though some of its congregation appear to have joined the Free Church rather than the United Secession Church in Waterside Street.

A small group of members of the Scottish Episcopal Church, who had been meeting in a room in the Brisbane Arms, took over the Relief Church and it became St Columba's Scottish Episcopal Church until the present church and a rectory were built in 1877. Thereafter the former Relief Church became St Columba's Hall and was used for functions and sporting activities until it was demolished at the turn of the century, when the area was cleared for the construction of the Sandringham flats.

For the Roman Catholic population in Largs, Mass was occasionally said; but from what period or how often is not known. In 1862, Largs became a separate mission under the care of the Rev. Joseph Small, although the first St Mary's Church in School Street, was not opened until 1870.

The Christian Brethren – sometimes known as the Plymouth Brethren because the movement, originating in Ireland, spread out over England and Scotland from Plymouth – made a considerable impact in Ayrshire in the mid-19th century. A group was formed in Largs in 1870, and met in the Bath Hall until they built their own meeting house, the Brisbane Hall, in 1929.

By the mid 19th century, therefore, an increasing number of the residents of Largs were committed to denominations outwith the Established Church. These bodies had their own separate history and traditions. Yet the territorial boundaries of the Parish were unchanged, and within them the Parish Minister was responsible for the spiritual care not only of his own Church members, but also those who had no religious affiliation.

JOHN KINROSS

Surprised and shocked by the extensive defections from its ranks, the Established Church set itself to recover. It had lost over one third of its ministers and even opponents of the Disruption admitted that amongst them were some of the most able and dedicated leaders of the Church. Yet the position was not as desperate as it might at first have seemed. Many of the parochial schoolmasters were qualified for the ministry, and not a few of them had remained "stickit ministers" only because they had failed to attract the attention of a patron. They could be drafted in to fill the 451 vacancies resulting from the Disruption and to replace serving ministers who, to improve their position or to escape from shattered relationships, wished to take advantage of the circumstances by moving to new parishes. In the general readjustment, Largs was particularly fortunate.

The vacancy following John Dow's demission was brief and the new minister was a young man of impeccable background and some experience.

The third son of a farmer named William Kinross, John Kinross was born on 13th July 1812 at Dunblane. There his mother's family had for nine successive generations worked the farm of Crosscaple on the Kippenross estate; and his grandfather, James Dawson, as an accepted authority on the planting of trees for a profitable return, had become the trusted adviser of several eminent landowners. John Kinross graduated Master of Arts of Glasgow University on 24th April 1833, and thereafter studied for two years at the Theological Hall in Edinburgh. He was licensed by the Presbytery of Dunblane on 2nd February 1836 and was employed as a tutor in various distinguished families, including that of the Earl of Glasgow, before being appointed in 1840, assistant to Dr John Campbell, Minister of Kilwinning. He was offered the Laigh Kirk of Kilmarnock by the Duke of Portland, but declined it; presumably because Sir John Gladstone of Fasque had already presented him to St Thomas's Church in Leith, to which he was inducted on 22nd June, 1842. He was there for little over a year, for on 7th July 1843 he was presented by Archibald William, Earl of Eglinton and Winton, to the Parish Church of Largs and was inducted on 1st September, 1843.

John Kinross was described as "a kind and scholarly gentleman, a vigorous and eloquent preacher, and a warm friend to missionary and educational movements" though it was added that he had "no love for new ideas or methods whether in creed or worship". He had wide interests, travelled extensively and was the author of two works: *A Holiday in Scandinavia* in 1871, and a pamphlet on *The Disestablishment of the Church of Scotland* in 1881. Both were published anonymously and even in Largs there is no trace of them. Although he never married, he was "given to hospitality" and played a leading part in the social life of his wealthier parishioners; though his "geniality" and "pawky humour" made him equally popular among the less affluent. It was perhaps significant of a desire to set aside recent controversy that for the first sermon he

preached in Largs he chose as his text verse two in the second chapter of First Corinthians:
"I am determined not to know anything among you save Jesus Christ and Him crucified".

But the Disruption could not be so easily ignored. The depleted Kirk Session had to be augmented, and among the prominent Largs men ordained as elders during the ministry of John Kinross were: David Glen, who became Session Clerk; George Scott of Auchengarth; John Robertson of Kilburn; Dr James Caskie, who served as Treasurer; Dr William Hunter of Woodbank; William Aiton, the schoolmaster; and John Carswell. The beadle was William Jamieson, who was succeeded in turn by William Jack and John Aitchison; though the designation of the post was changed to the more modern "officer". The church door collections of the Established Churches, already hard pressed before the Disruption, were no longer adequate for the relief of local poverty and, by the Poor Law Amendment Act of 1845, this responsibility passed to public bodies with the right to assess property holders.

At the outset of his ministry John Kinross was much concerned about the few Fairlie people who had remained members of the Parish Church. The Chapel of Ease was closed for almost a year and it was not until June 1844 that the Rev. James Clark, formerly assistant at Kilwinning, was inducted as minister with John Kinross giving him and his small congregation every encouragement and support. The need for a similar small church in the northern part of the parish was recognised, but there was some disagreement as to the most suitable site for it. The minister of Inverkip favoured the Meigle and complained that in estimating the population of Kellybridge – as Skelmorlie was then known – John Kinross had inflated his figures by including the crew of a yacht anchored offshore, and a group of drainers and road builders temporarily working in the area. Perhaps each of the reverend gentlemen thought the further the new place of worship was from his own church, the fewer of his outlying members would defect to it. Eventually the Presbytery decided on Skelmorlie, and the Rev. Walter L G Boyd was inducted as minister of the newly built Kellybridge Chapel of Ease on 21st August, 1856.

Nationally it had become clear that reform of the historic parish structure was essential. The Church was given permission to erect *quoad sacra* parishes provided that for each an endowment of £120 per annum was secured in advance; and by the end of the century more than 400 new parishes had come into being. Skelmorlie quickly fulfilled the condition, and in 1860 Kellybridge Chapel of Ease became Skelmorlie Parish Church. In view of the reluctance of John Kinross to condone change in the forms of worship, it is of some interest that Walter Boyd had an organ installed in his church in Skelmorlie. It is said locally that it was used before its official authorisation by the Presbytery of Greenock on 21st June 1865, and this, if true, would give it some claim to have been the first organ in use for public worship by the Established Church: an event usually credited to Edinburgh Greyfriars on 22nd April, 1865.

Fairlie took longer to secure the necessary endowment, and in the meantime Largs Church made small grants towards its expenses and the salary of the Parish Church schoolmaster. However, on 19th May 1876, the petition was presented to the Commissioners for the Plantation of Kirks requesting that the Chapel of Ease become Fairlie Parish Church.

As a result of the erection of these two *quoad sacra* parishes, the Parish of Largs proper was greatly reduced in size, extending only from the northern boundary of Kelburn Estate to the Blackhouse Burn. Although the parish was smaller, the number of parishioners had increased. The town of Largs was growing steadily. In addition, the Greenock Railway Company had reached Wemyss Bay in 1865. This made it possible for business men to travel daily to the city and there was quite an influx of wealthy merchants, especially to the northern edge of the town. It was for Largs an era of prosperity and mounting civic pride. By the 19th century, the administrative machinery of the early burghs had broken down completely and in 1876 Largs took advantage of an Act of Parliament that allowed "populous places" to elect representatives with power to raise money for various public services. Both Robert Aitken, the first Provost of Largs, and his successor Major Alexander Haldane Eckford, were active members of the Parish Church.

Freed from the pressure of material care for the poor, the Church could turn its attention to more spiritual matters. Missionary work abroad and evangelism at home were encouraged. There was no serious attempt to introduce a formal liturgy but there were efforts to make services more orderly and reverent, and in them to concentrate on worship rather than instruction. Higher standards of culture and refinement in the private lives of the upper classes led to a wish to make church buildings and furnishings less austere, and in 1869 the General Assembly appointed a Committee on Christian Life and Work to assess and promote social work in the individual parishes. John Kinross had little sympathy for innovations in worship but his pastoral activities were not inconsistent with the new developments in the Church. His involvement in the work of the National Bible Society was even carried to the length of taking with him a small supply of Bibles for distribution on his foreign tours. He was keenly interested in promoting due observance of "the sancity of the Lord's Day", and he was prepared to accept a moderate degree of embellishment in his Church. Shortly before his death, he commented to a friend on "the marked improvement he was able to recognise in the habit and tone of society" and especially on "the great change for the better in the general abolition of the old drinking customs in connection with funerals". Certainly, throughout his ministry he was quick to see and to support any opportunities for social improvement in the community. In 1844 he was largely responsible for the inauguration of the Female School of Industry, which in 1852 moved to premises afterwards known as the Parish Council Chambers. It was intended to provide for girls from working class backgrounds a suitable education under the supervision of the Kirk Session and a ladies' committee. In 1852 when Miss Hutcheson from Aberdeen was appointed teacher, the Session agreed to install grates and gas fittings in the rooms provided for her private use, the cost to be charged against the fund for heating the church and buying requisites for the Sunday School. According to local tradition, the school day began very properly with prayers at which the pupils reverently bowed their heads – but did not close their eyes as they were expected to combine their devotions with their sewing.

The Female School of Industry fulfilled its function for almost fifty years, although during that time the Church largely lost its influence over education. The abolition of theological tests in all faculties other than divinity, severed the close link that had existed between the Universities and the Church; and by the Education (Scotland) Act of 1872, responsibility for primary education passed by law to elected school boards. Both the Established Church and the Free Church insisted that in the state schools, religious instruction "as of use and wont" would be given to all pupils except those whose parents objected; and so, on the whole, a friendly relationship was maintained with the new schools. Largs School Board was duly elected and took over the management of the Parish Church School in School Street and the Brisbane Academy in Lade Street, which had been the Free Church School. Beyond the classroom John Kinross helped organise a "Mechanics Library". He may well have been relieved when it moved from its first location – "the principal room of the public house of Mr Peter Hendry" – though he probably deplored the fact that thereafter it was "constantly in search of a home". Nevertheless, it was conceded that a worthwhile collection of books and periodicals had been built up for the use of those who could not afford to buy them. Some years ago a very old man in Fairlie recalled that as a boy he had earned a small sum of pocket money by walking into Largs on Saturdays to change his father's book.

Stained glass windows were installed in the Parish Church. On the east wall were two presented in 1865 by "Hugh Morris Lang Esq." and "Robert Kerr Esq.", the latter adding to its inscription "This Church was erected in 1812 A.D. John Mitchell, M.D., Minister". The three on the north wall were the gifts of "John Lang, Esq."; of "James Dunlop Esq.,1865"; and of "Thomas McCunn, Esq.". The corresponding windows on the south wall were "Erected in memory of beloved relatives by Mrs Ramsay, Greenock"; "The gift of Mr and Mrs Stewart, St Fillans, 1866"; and "Erected by Mrs Moon in memory of a beloved mother".

An article on the Church in the *Largs and Millport Weekly News* of 16th May 1885, though it refers to them as "fine stained glass

windows", gives no description other than that "in a measure they redeem the inside from painful plainess", as did a mural tablet of white marble commemorating Sir Thomas Brisbane who died on 27th January 1860. It was placed near the pulpit and consisted of
> "a medallion vignette in half relief of the great soldier and scientist surrounded with the instruments of the callings he so greatly adorned", and had been presented by the officers of the 34th Regiment, "in grateful remembrance of the deep and active interest he at all times evinced in the welfare of every individual connected with the corps".

In the eighties, a new field of social concern presented itself. The railway was slowly making its way northwards from Ardrossan. It brought into the district squads of navvies, and John Kinross was prominent among those who tried to improve their rough living conditions. Accommodation was secured in "part of the bakery and granary premises" in Main Street for reading and recreation rooms, and "a respectable and intelligent woman" was placed in charge. At the opening ceremony on 6th April 1883, "there was a good attendance of the men and boys engaged about the line"; and following "a plentiful and tasteful supper" supplied by Mr MacKay the baker, at the expense of the Misses Lang of Warren Park, there was a concert. The main part of the entertainment was given by members of the Parish Church choir but one or two of the railway workers also contributed to the programme: one performing Irish, and another "patriotic Polish" songs. John Kinross was chairman, and combining two of his interests, announced that he had put some Bibles on the table and he would be happy if any workman who did not already possess a Bible of his own would accept one as a gift from him. He also could not resist making
> "the good singing of two of the navvies he had just heard the opportunity for addressing a few words...on the elevating and humanising influence of cultivating a love of flowers and music".

John Kinross left the function early. No reason was given but he was already in failing health. A few years earlier he had suffered what seems to have been a slight stroke and it had to some extent impaired his physical ability. He had perhaps never been very robust, for over the years there were vague references to his illness, and throughout his ministry he was helped in his parochial duties by a series of assistants. It was held to be no small part of his professional achievement that he furthered the training of so many able young men for the work of the ministry. Among them were: Rev. James Stewart, Minister of Wilton, Hawick until 1886, Rev. Robert Turner, Minister of Kinettles until 1893, Rev. Alexander Inglis, Minister of Kilmaurs for many years, Rev. John Reid, Minister of Crail until 1917, Rev. James Caven, Minister of Kirkintilloch until 1893, Rev. John Yuille, Minister of Gourock, 1875-1879, Rev. Daniel Cogswell, later of the Church of England, Rev. James Kidd, Minister of Bressay until 1894, Rev. James Mitchell, Minister of Norrieston until 1926, Rev. Robert Cameron, Minister of Armadale until 1909, Rev. David Baird, in 1928 a minister in Australia, Rev. Thomas Smith Goldie, Minister of Granton until 1927.

At a congregational meeting on 13th January 1877, John Kinross intimated that he would be prepared to forego £100 per annum from his stipend if the Church would augment this into a salary sufficient to employ a new assistant in the more permanent capacity of his future successor. There was a good deal of confused talk and not a little acrimony, for some of those present could see no reason to employ two men to do the work of one and contended that either they got a new minister or they did not. In the end no decision was reached and John Kinross remained in sole charge of the Largs Church until his death, at the age of 71, on Wednesday 5th December, 1883.

The funeral was held on the following Monday. The shops and businesses in Largs closed as a mark of respect; steamers calling at the pier flew their flags at half mast; and the Church was crowded with representatives of all denominations and public bodies in the town, and with a host of friends and colleagues of the dead minister. The coffin was carried from the Church by members of the Largs Battery of the Ayrshire and Galloway Volunteers, to which John Kinross had been chaplain since its inception some twenty years earlier. The Volunteers and most of the congregation followed the hearse on foot as far as the Noddle Bridge. From there a long line of private carriages went on to Wemyss Bay station, and it was remarked that, although the weather was wet and very stormy, there were many ladies in the cortege. John Kinross was buried at Dunblane and there is a memorial tablet to him in Dunblane Cathedral.

On the next Sunday, memorial services were held in a Parish Church where the galleries were draped in black and most of the congregation were dressed in mourning. Tributes to John Kinross were paid in the Free Church, the United Presbyterian Church, and in Millport. The addresses were reported in some detail in the local press and under the florid style of the time there ran a real feeling of esteem and even affection.

JOHN KEITH

The death of John Kinross brought a new experience for Largs Parish Church but, as the *Largs and Millport Weekly News* was later to comment, "it cannot be said to have been altogether a pleasant one". Patronage had finally been abolished in 1874. The church courts were in charge of rules for the election and confirmation of a new minister, but choice of the person to be appointed lay with the congregation.

The procedure seemed simple enough. The Presbytery of Greenock appointed the Rev. John Keith, Minister of Skelmorlie, as Interim Moderator; the congregation elected a committee to consider suitable applicants and the Kirk Session drew up a list of communicants and adherents entitled to vote. The committee deliberated but failed to arrive at any conclusion.

A second committee produced a short leet which was finally reduced to two; and at a congregational meeting on 2nd June 1884, the Rev. Mr Hutcheson of Coatbridge was elected by 136 votes to 121. But supporters of the defeated candidate refused to accept the majority decision and flooded the Presbytery with objections. Mr Hutcheson, seeing little future for himself in such a hopelessly divided congregation, withdrew his application and the whole process had to begin again. A third committee was appointed, but by that time few ministers were willing to embroil themselves in the affair. Eventually a compromise was reached. John Keith was thought to have acquitted himself well in difficult circumstances and had made himself quite popular with his fractious charges. The congregation took the unusual step of presenting their call to the Interim Moderator and the Presbytery, no doubt relieved to escape from a problem that was fast becoming insoluble, agreed to his appointment. Inevitably there was a good deal of puerile humour on the subject of John Keith being "transported" from Skelmorlie to Largs.

On the afternoon of Saturday 10th January 1885, a curious little ceremony took place at Underbank[21], the Holms-Kerr residence. It was emphasised that this was not a congregational function but simply a recognition by "a few friends" of the "onerous nature of the duties" undertaken by David Glen, the Session Clerk, during "the protracted vacancy". Mrs Holms-Kerr presented a silver claret jug and a purse of sovereigns to him. She did not fail to point out that both she and her husband had voted against John Keith but that, though disappointed at not getting their choice she hoped that everyone would "sink self and their own little differences and help the minister". Her forbearance and Christian charity were widely commended by her friends and by all who wished to curry favour with one of the more influential families in the district.

The son of John Keith of the Scottish Education Department, and Margaret Russell, the Rev. John Keith was born at Edinburgh on 14th December, 1850. He was dux medallist of Edinburgh High School and had a distinguished academic career at Edinburgh University, where he graduated Master of Arts and Bachelor of Divinity in 1877, having acted as an assistant to Professor John Stuart Blackie of the Department of Greek from 1871 to 1877. Licensed by the Presbytery of Edinburgh on 26th July 1876, he became assistant minister in St Mary's Church, Edinburgh. He was ordained in Skelmorlie Parish Church on 7th November 1878, and served there for just over six years before being translated to Largs.

John Keith was a bachelor whose unmarried sister kept house for him. Throughout his life he retained a keen interest in Greek studies and from time to time corresponded with friends in that language.

He was Clerk to the Presbytery of Greenock from 1888 to 1901 and although he strongly upheld the principles of the Established Church, he was on excellent terms with the local clergymen of other denominations. His preaching was said to be "mature, sound and thoughtful" but in a letter to him on 18th June 1887, the Clerk to the Heritors wrote acidly,

> "I duly received your letter of 14th curt. which is as prolix and pointless as most of your sermons".

The charge may, or may not, have been true but, whatever his preaching abilities, there can be no doubt that John Keith organised and extended the work of both Church and Parish and was anxious to increase the dignity of his services, though not always without opposition from his more reactionary parishioners. The epitaph to Sir Christopher Wren – "Si monumentum requiris circumspice" – has over the years become rather hackneyed but it can with considerable truth be applied to him. The Church as it stands today owes much to his determination and outstanding qualities of leadership.

The induction was fixed for Thursday, 5th February 1885. On Wednesday the bellman on his rounds announced that the following day would be observed as a public holiday and all the shops would be closed. He had immediately to retrace his steps with a correction: the United Presbyterian shops would remain open. There is no record as to how the Free Church shops reacted.

The induction service was held in the afternoon and after it ninety gentlemen – office-bearers and guests – gathered in the Artillery Hall for a dinner at which the menu and the toast list were equally impressive. In the evening the "Induction Soiree" held in the Church took the customary course. There were speeches, tea, presentations to the incoming minister, and sacred music and solos, which Miss Houston, in the words of the local press, accompanied on the pianoforte "carefully, correctly and judiciously". But for the audience the most interesting item on the programme must have been the intimation made by John Keith:

> "As I indicated at the dinner, not only has the hand of welcome been extended but the hand of munificence has also been extended. A long-felt want in this parish and congregation has been that of a hall pertaining to the

church. A few days ago I received intimation from the legal representatives of a member of this congregation, who is unable to be here tonight, that she intends to provide a hall for the Church. I mean that venerable lady, Mrs Stewart of St Fillans".

Elizabeth Stewart died in Glasgow on 14th March 1886 in her 86th year. Most of her estate was bequeathed to various schemes of the Established Church but the money she had assigned to Largs Church was more than enough to erect a handsome church hall. Five years passed before it was completed. The main hall, to which access was gained by an imposing outside stair, was spacious with a platform at one end and wooden panels which could be swung out from the walls to give each of the Sunday School classes some measure of privacy. The various offices on the ground floor included a vestry, a library, and a session room large enough to serve on occasion as a lesser hall. Mrs Buchanan of Craigneish presented "an excellent harmonium" for use in the hall. Mrs Moon of Broomfields donated £50 for the purchase of books and the Misses Orr of Volo Villa and Mrs Hill of Main Street also provided books. Some years later, portraits of the late Mr and Mrs Stewart were presented to be hung in the building. John Keith was ill and unable to be present when Elizabeth Stewart's trustees officially handed the hall over at its formal opening on Tuesday, 11th August, 1891. Before the month was out the Stewart Memorial Hall had demonstrated its usefulness in the Parish. An elaborate three-day bazaar raised the sum of £615 though not for any purpose of the Parish Church. It had been organised by the Free Church to set up a fund for the maintenance of their organ.

The Rev. Mr Milne of Gourock in his exhortation to the new minister at the induction service had urged him to "make preaching his main work". Yet in the early years of his ministry at Largs, sermons can hardly have been John Keith's chief preoccupation. There were many changes. The Manse was over a century old and for many years had required frequent repair. In June 1885 the decision was made that it would be less expensive to rebuild it completely on the same site at an estimated cost of £2,000. The architect chosen was Allan Stevenson of Ayr. George Barclay, a Largs builder, was appointed Master of Works and the most competent tradesmen of Largs, Skelmorlie, and Millport were contracted to carry out the work.[22] The heritors agreed to add an additional sum of £87 for gas fittings, grates, and blinds and John Keith himself undertook to cover the costs of painting and papering.

As a result of John Keith's more modern outlook innovations in worship, resisted by John Kinross, came rapidly. The first edition of the *Scottish Hymnal* had been authorised by the General Assembly in 1870. Largs Church introduced its use in 1885 so that the praise was enriched by hymns in addition to the Metrical Psalms and Paraphrases, and at the same time the Church introduced the "Change of Postures". Formerly the congregation had stood during prayers and remained seated when singing. The more modern practice was to stand during the praise and to sit, or kneel, in prayer. In the same year new-fangled Communion Cards replaced the old tokens and the hour of the second diet of worship was changed from the afternoon to 6 pm.

Alterations finally completed in 1883 had transformed the High Kirk of Edinburgh into a dignified setting for civic and national ceremonial. There were those who held that the Parish Churches, each in its own district, should fulfil the same function on a lesser scale. It was in this climate of opinion that, as the Stewart Memorial Hall rose alongside the Church, the decision was made to embark on an even more ambitious project. The Parish Church was simple, old-fashioned and too small, especially in the summer months when Largs was crowded with holidaymakers. It must be rebuilt in a style more suited to the part it ought to play in the life of the community. The heritors made three conditions: that the costs would be met without call on them except for such personal donations as they might choose to make; that they would have no liability for the upkeep of the new building; and that they as heritors would have allocated to them as many "sittings" in the new Church as they had held by law in its predecessor. By accepting these provisions the Largs congregation took what was for the time an unusual step. The Parish Church would no longer be dependent on legally bound heritors but would be built and maintained by the voluntary efforts of its own people.

By 1889 two important decisions had been made: first to have instrumental music in the new Church and second to start on the demolition of the existing Church. The stones were used as infill for the Hollow in Bath Street, preparatory to laying the foundations of the new United Presbyterian Church which was to replace the old building in Waterside Street. By invitation of the Rev. Charles Watson and his Kirk Session, the Parish Church congregation met for worship in the Free Church. This arrangement had the added advantage that, as they went to and from their services, they could, without displaying too much vulgar curiosity, carefully observe the building of the United Presbyterians' new Church and compare its progress with that of their own.

The new Parish Church was designed by a young architect named Andrew Balfour of the Glasgow firm of Steel and Balfour. The plan was cruciform with galleries over the entrance and both transepts, and was so laid out that the Stewart Memorial Hall would become complementary to it on the north and east. The original estimate of the cost of building was between £15,000 and £20,000. In the event it slightly exceeded the latter figure. A grant of £1,000 was received from the Baird Trust of the Scottish Church but apart from that all the money was raised from members and friends since the leading heritors, being non-resident, made no contribution. Today in the Church a bronze mural tablet in memory of Robert Kerr Holms-Kerr and his wife Margaret Ralston carries the inscription

"Without their munificence this House of God provided by the offerings of the people could not have been completed".

Robert Holms-Kerr of Underbank was senior partner in the Glasgow firm of stockbrokers Holms-Kerr and Hedderwick. He was a descendant of that William Kerr who brought the bell for the 1812 Church to Largs, but he was to make a much greater contribution than his ancestor towards building a new Church in Largs. From the outset he enthusiastically supported the idea of rebuilding and was appointed Convener of the Building Committee. It was later estimated that the various branches of the Holms-Kerr families donated almost one third of the total cost of building and furnishing the Church and it was only because Robert Holms-Kerr legally absolved the heritors from all liability by standing as personal guarantor of any deficit on the completed building that the work was able to begin when it did. In 1891 the congregation moved for worship into the newly opened Stewart Memorial Hall and so could watch the progress of the building under the supervision of John Gardner, the Inspector of Works. He lived in Largs for two years and became a popular figure in the town. When he left on completion of his work, Halkhill Bowling Club held a farewell supper for him in the Eglinton Hotel and presented him with silver-mounted bowls and a gold pendant for his wife.

The Church was built of red sandstone brought from the Ballochmyle Quarries. In the congregational rivalry with the United Presbyterians as to which would reach the nearer to heaven, the Parish Church made a noble effort with a spire 150 feet high. For it, a clock with Westminster chimes and four illuminated dials was presented by Alexander Muir of Broomfields House, whose family had been among the first regular summer visitors to Largs and who had retired to the town after many years as a merchant in South America.

The large windows of the galleries were all of stained glass. That in the west gallery, above the Church entrance, was the work of Messrs Cottier of London and was presented by Mrs Moon, formerly Margaret Anne Buchanan. The central light, which depicts Christ with the little children, carries the inscription:

> "To the Glory of God erected by Mrs William Moon Broomfields in Largs Parish Church rebuilt 1891".

It is sometimes thought to have been the Moon window from the 1812 Church but the reference is to the rebuilding of the Church, not the window. The light on the left which portrays Christ by the well talking with the Samarian woman is dedicated to the memory of Margaret Moon's first husband John Spreul, who died on 13th March 1845, and their two children – James, who died in 1844 aged 15, and Joanna in 1841, aged 12. The light on the right portrays Christ visiting the home at Bethany and is dedicated to Margaret Moon's second husband William Moon, who died on 5th August 1873. Margaret Moon did not live to see the window completed. She died on 4th August 1891 aged 86.

The window of the south gallery was the gift of a member of the Holms-Kerr family. Designed and made by Alfred Webster of the Stephen Adam Studio in Glasgow, it represents a Te Deum on the Work of Man. It was planned by Margaret Lang Hoggan, the wife of George B Hoggan a prominent Glasgow lawyer, as a memorial of her mother Elizabeth Kerr who married William Kerr of Brabloch, Paisley; and her two maiden aunts the Misses Margaret and Elizabeth Kerr of Rosebank, Largs. Rosebank had been the home of the Kerr family, and though the Hoggans lived in Glasgow, much of their life was spent in Largs, at Rosebank. Margaret Hoggan, too, died before the window was finished but the Kerr Trust took over responsibility for its completion.

William McCunn of Landour presented the north gallery window in memory of his parents. Appropriately enough for a keen yachtsman, it grouped together incidents from the Gospels dealing with the sea – Christ walking on the water; the terrified disciples in the storm; the miraculous draught of fishes. It was the work of Messrs Wingfield of Birmingham.

As the new Church slowly took shape, enthusiasm mounted. The congregation resolved that the interior furnishings and decoration should equal the impressive exterior. Little was carried over from the old Church. Parts of the ornamental windows had been incorporated into the Stewart Memorial Hall, the massive Communion chair was to serve in the vestry, and the commemorative tablet to Sir Thomas Brisbane was to find a new place at the east end of the north aisle. But a host of gifts large and small came to enhance the Church. It would be impossible to list them all, but some record should be made of those that gave, and still give, the Church much of its character and of the donors, many of them almost forgotten.

Robert Holms-Kerr presented a pipe organ. He consulted the organist of Glasgow Cathedral, Dr A L Peace, who specified an instrument of two manuals and pedals from the celebrated London firm of Henry Willis and Sons. The oak organ casing was constructed to the architect's design by John Craig of Pollokshields, who added a matching prayer desk as his own personal gift. The octagonal oak pulpit with carved panels representing the Parables of Our Lord, is based on that in Norwich Cathedral and was made by Miles S Gibson of Glasgow. It was the gift of Isabella Wilkie in memory of her husband James Wilkie of Acre. A native of Uddingston, he became agent of the Royal Bank of Scotland in Largs and took an active part in local affairs being, along with Major Eckford, one of the first two magistrates appointed when Largs became a police burgh in 1876.

The Scotts of Barr and Thirdpart presented an oak Communion table in memory of their father George Scott of Auchengarth, who had been an elder in the Church for many years. The Communion chair in Austrian oak was the gift of J C Bryce, a local cabinetmaker, who carved it to his own design based on the west gable of the Church. The lectern, a bronze eagle on an onyx pedestal, was presented by Richard Brown of Haylie. Margaret Holms-Kerr presented a font of various marbles in the name of her children as a memorial to John Kinross who had baptised them. Also in memory of John Kinross, Mrs Ramsay and Miss Ewan of Woodbank presented a set of Communion silver. A brass almsdish was presented by Rankine Orr of Volo Villa and his sisters; a pulpit Bible, Psalter, and Hymnal by Mrs J R McColl of Bath Street; collection bags by Mrs Stirling of The Knowe; and a pulpit cushion by Mrs James Houston of Bath Street. And in the spate of gifts, not all were for the Church. Mr and Mrs George Baird of Planetree presented an elaborate clock for the Stewart Memorial Hall as an appreciation of the work of the Sunday School. By July 1892 – only four weeks after the formal opening of the new United Presbyterian Church, which was to be known as Clark Memorial Church – the Parish Church was completed.

On Thursday 14th a few loose ends from the old Church were tidied up at a function in the Stewart Memorial Hall when various presentations were made. Robert Beck, on officially demitting office as the last Precentor of the Parish Church, was given a gold watch and a case of gold studs. Miss Houston, a local music teacher, who had introduced instrumental music into the Services by playing the harmonium in the church hall, was given a silver tea service. Naturally she was too bashful and ladylike to speak in public and so delegated David Glen, the Session Clerk, to express her thanks. On the other hand, Margaret Holms-Kerr was sufficiently emancipated to speak for herself. In handing over a clock to John Keith she advised him to wind it regularly so that it would not run down as he himself had become run down by the worries of bringing his new Church into existence.

The Church was dedicated on Friday, 15th July. The Rev. J F McPherson of Greenock conducted the Service; The Very Rev. James McGregor BD, of St Cuthbert's Edinburgh, preached and Dr Peace played the organ.

At the beginning of the ceremony Mr and Mrs Robert Holms-Kerr laid a commemoration stone in the chancel. It contained coins, current issues of the *Glasgow Herald,* the *Scotsman* and the *Largs and Millport Weekly News* and a record of the planning of the Church with a list of the names of all who had contributed in any way towards it. Eleven elders signed this statement. They were: David Glen, Senior Elder and Session Clerk; Dr William Caskie; Major Alexander Eckford of Elmbank; Robert Robertson of Dykes, who had all held office for many years; Robert Beck; Thomas Duff; William Duff; Robert Houston; William Mackie; John Rodger; and Hugh Scott, who had been more recently ordained. After the Service there was a sumptuous luncheon party in the Stewart Memorial Hall. It was provided by Robert Holms- Kerr, who had engaged the Queen's Restaurant Company of Glasgow as caterers. In the speeches a good deal of lip service was paid to the part that the women of the congregation had played in achieving the new Church, but the function was strictly limited to gentlemen. Perhaps the ladies were permitted to have a snack in some obscure anteroom? In the evening, and again on Saturday evening, Dr Peace gave organ recitals which, as he pointed out in his programme notes, were designed "to exhibit the resources of the instrument in its purely musical and artistic phase" although it would in future be more properly "subordinated to the sacred character of the Service". The Rev. John Macleod DD of Govan conducted the morning Service on Sunday 17th before what was described as the largest congregation ever assembled in Largs, though even then quite a few people had been unable to gain admittance to the crowded Church. John Keith himself took the evening Service and on the following Sunday Communion Services brought the opening celebrations to a close.

Some time later the *Largs and Millport Weekly News* reported the solemnisation of the first wedding in the new Parish Church. On Friday 2nd June 1893, Miss Kate Houston[23] was married to Mr William Wilton of Glasgow, who was "not unknown to fame as the match secretary of the Glasgow Rangers Football Club". The article ends with an interesting comment on changing social customs,
> "We understand there was never a marriage celebrated in the old parish church on the site of which the present handsome building stands".

It was often said of John Keith that the strain of overseeing a new Manse, a new Hall and a new Church so undermined his constitution that he was no longer the same force in his later years. Though probably not for the reason given, he did have a serious illness soon after the Church was completed and was never again in really good health. Yet there is nothing to suggest that he was unable to direct the less dramatic but steady progress of his Church. He brightened and dignified his Sunday Services by encouraging the choir to include Anthems and Prose Psalms and, greatly daring, in 1893 he introduced a Service on Christmas Day. Gradually over the years the old ways changed. The Thursday Fast Day had become virtually obsolete and was allowed to lapse, while discipline cases disappeared from the records. In 1892 a Boys' Brigade Company was formed; Sales of Work in aid of foreign missions were held and a Ladies' Committee of Management was formed to run the Parish Library.

John Keith was helped in his parochial work by assistants – the Rev. John Heggie, the Rev. James H Gillespie and the Rev. Andrew MacFarlane – but the congregation also played a part in the Church's outreach. As part of a national attempt to bring the Church closer to farm servants, there were on Sunday afternoons, frequent cottage meetings in outlying parts of the Parish; and at them Robert Beck, who had become a stalwart member of the choir, led the singing. Earlier in the century the Kirk Session had minuted that the date of their meeting had been intimated to all members who were not dead. No doubt this eminently sensible practice was continued. In 1892 they appointed a Works Committee with Major Eckford as its first convener, succeeded by John Rodger. Church office-bearers of today may find it ironic that for very many years the dearest ambition of this Committee was that the Fabric Fund they instituted would attain a capital of £1,000. David Glen died in October 1901. Whatever services he rendered to the Church, local historians will not easily forgive him for the fact that the 18th century Church records he claimed to have "discovered" vanished forever with his death. James Watson followed him as Session Clerk.

Largs Public School, designed by T Graham Abercromby, the architect of Clark Memorial Church, was built at the Shotts Park. It had not been completed in May 1893, but the School Board had furnishing from the Parish and Free Church schools hastily transferred to it in a frantic attempt to forestall HM Inspector, who on his previous visit to Largs had reported adversely on the old school buildings and threatened to have the government grant reduced if there was no improvement. Pupils from both schools attended for the first time on Monday, 22nd May. The opening ceremonies were necessarily informal and curtailed because workmen were still in the building, but Largs was much impressed by the dignity given to the occasion by the headmaster, James Arthur "arrayed in his gown as a Master of Arts".

The new public school had been designed to accommodate all the children of the district. The Female School of Industry, despite its humble origins, had become popular and frequently was forced to refuse intending pupils because of overcrowding. The Kirk Session decided to take advantage of the approaching marriage of the headmistress, Miss Lyon, by handing over its management to the School Board. The pupils assembled as usual on Monday, 5th June 1893, and in the presence of what was described as an "influential deputation", the last prizegiving was held. Presentations were made to the staff and the Female School of Industry was formally closed. In the afternoon, under the command of Miss A L Smith, the assistant mistress who had been appointed to a post in the public school, "the children were marched up to the new school, where they were enrolled...and assigned their class work at once".

But the old school buildings had still many years of service to the community ahead of them. The old Parish Church School became the Roman Catholic School and the Female School of Industry housed a succession of minor local government offices. James Stevenson of Haylie bought the Brisbane Academy and handed it over in trust as the Stevenson Institute for the cultural and educational use of the people of Largs. At last the Mechanics' Library had found a permanent home.

John Keith contributed a translation of the *Epistles of Clement of Rome* to Clark's Ante-Nicene Library and, chiefly as a result of this work, the University of Edinburgh conferred on him the honorary degree of Doctor of Divinity in April 1901. His health had deteriorated so much that in March 1902 the Presbytery of Greenock granted him six months leave of absence. Although his illness was not thought to be fatal he died at Perth on 3rd June 1902, in his 52nd year. Representatives from Largs attended his burial at Warriston Cemetery in Edinburgh on the afternoon of Saturday, 6th June. In Largs at the time of the funeral, the shops were closed, the bells of all the churches were tolled and a Service was held in the Parish Church with pulpit and galleries draped in black. On the following Sunday there was no Service. It was then the custom for relatives of a serving minister to have the Services in his church conducted on the Sunday following his death by one of his personal friends. Owing to a series of misunderstandings, Miss Keith had made no arrangements. It was pointed out that this was quite in accordance with precedent, for the same thing had happened on the Sunday immediately following the death of John Kinross.

In October 1902, Miss Keith presented to the Church a portrait she had painted of her brother, and in 1904 the congregation erected on the east wall of the vestibule, a marble tablet commemorating him.

GAVIN LANG PAGAN

While Largs was mourning John Keith, arrangements were going forward to celebrate the coronation of King Edward VII. Coronation Day, 26th June 1902, was declared a public holiday and shopkeepers and householders were urged to decorate their premises with flags and bunting. The first event in the official programme was divine service in the Parish Church at 11 am. At noon the bells of all the churches would be rung; representatives of the local trades and societies would take part in a procession round the town headed by bands; the Alexandra Esplanade, which carried the shore pathway from the pier to the Gogo, would be formally opened; the Town Council and leading citizens would meet for a civic luncheon in the Victoria Hotel; in the afternoon, sports would be held on the north green and in the evening a host of private parties had been planned, ranging from banquets to modest suppers, for which many people had laid in stores of fireworks. And then between 1 and 2 o'clock on Tuesday, 24th June, ex-Provost Watson received a devastating "telephone message". The Coronation had been cancelled! Later in the day the newspapers arrived to confirm the rumour. The King was seriously ill. His subjects could only await the outcome of a major operation and all thought of rejoicing must be abandoned.

The Alexandra Esplanade was already in use, so a perfunctory opening ceremony was held on Tuesday 8th July, though the commemorative plaque laid that day carried the date 26th June. The Coronation, abbreviated because of the King's convalescence, took place in August but the local celebrations had lost much of their initial enthusiasm. Some attempt was made to decorate shops and houses; steamers were dressed overall, railway engines were ornamented with flags and flowers but there was no public holiday and most of the planned events were postponed until the customary autumn holiday in September. Even the official church service attracted no more than "a fair attendance".

In the meantime the Parish Church had been choosing its new minister. The Vacancy Committee considered many likely candidates but, profiting from the experience of the past, chose only one nominee and took the precaution that he was a man whom the congregation could hardly refuse.

Voting took place in the Stewart Memorial Hall on the afternoon and evening of Tuesday, 30th September 1902. At 9 pm. the votes were counted. Three people, through ignorance or ill-will, had spoiled their papers; 32 had demonstrated their independence by voting against; but 322 had approved the Committee's choice. At about 9.30 p m., attended by the Kirk Session, the Rev. J McGilchrist of Skelmorlie, who was Interim Moderator, announced from the steps at the main door of the Church that subject to Presbyterial confirmation, the Rev. Gavin Lang Pagan had been elected Parish Minister of Largs.

Gavin Lang Pagan was born on 13th April, 1873. On both sides of his family he was related to outstanding churchmen. His father, the Very Rev. John Pagan DD, was Minister of Bothwell and had been Moderator of the General Assembly in 1899. His mother was Margaret Wiseman, daughter of the Rev. Gavin Lang of Glasford. Her brother, the Rev. John Marshall Lang, as a young man was censured by the Presbytery of Aberdeen for having made the outrageous suggestion that his congregation in the East Kirk of Aberdeen should stand when singing. He did, however, survive the disgrace to become minister of the Barony Church in Glasgow and subsequently Principal of Aberdeen University. His son, Cosmo Gordon Lang, after a distinguished academic career at Glasgow University and Balliol College, became a notable clergyman in the Anglican Church. He was Archbishop of York when his cousin was minister of Largs and was enthroned as Archbishop of Canterbury in November 1928.

Educated at Hamilton Academy and Glasgow University, Gavin Lang Pagan graduated Master of Arts in 1893 and Bachelor of Divinity in 1896. He was licensed by the Presbytery of Hamilton on 29th September 1896, and served as assistant in Abbotshall, Kirkcaldy; Rosemount, Aberdeen; and St Cuthbert's, Edinburgh; before being ordained at Callander on 7th September, 1899. He was minister there for three years before being translated to Largs.

The Induction was held on 26th November 1902 and, as was to

Group showing the Minister and elders, taken in 1889, outside the old Largs Parish Church, immediately prior to the demolition of the building to make way for the erection of the present Church. Left to right: Mr Steele, Architect for new church; John Watson; James Patrick; Major Eckford; R. K. Holms-Kerr; Rev. Dr. John Keith; David Glen, Session Clerk; Mr Crockett, Auchenames; John Robertson.

be expected from the new minister's background, there was a distinguished clerical gathering. Largs had the pleasure of welcoming an ex-Moderator in the person of Gavin Pagan's father and also the distinction of being among the first to congratulate his cousin, the Rev. J Gillespie of Mouswald, who had just been appointed Moderator Elect of the 1903 Assembly. After the Service, Robert Holms-Kerr entertained a large party of gentlemen to dinner in the Stewart Memorial Hall and by that time Thomas MacKay was sufficiently established to be allowed to cater for it. In the evening a large representation of the congregation met for tea in the hall, and at 8 o'clock moved into the Church which was open to the public for the customary programme of speeches, presentations, and music. A few points stand out from the slightly fulsome spate of oratory that distinguished the day. Gavin Pagan's colleagues felt that he was to be congratulated on having practically everything that a minister could wish for: a magnificent church; a modern manse; a virtually unanimous call and a parish that comprised both town and country and both rich and poor. Dr John Pagan recalled that in his own first parish his predecessor and the Free Church minister, both excellent men, for sixteen years had not even so much as shaken hands with each other and he was therefore delighted to see the friendly relationship that existed between the churches in his son's parish.

Dr Charles Watson of St John's added that in his experience of almost 40 years in Largs he could not remember any unkind feelings between the ministers and congregations of the various local churches. Dr Watson may have been guilty of some exaggeration, but Largs does seem to have had little of the bitter controversies that raged elsewhere for the guests at the function included not only the United Free Church ministers, but also Canon Low of the Episcopal Church and Father Murray who had recently arrived in Largs.

In his own remarks Gavin Pagan pointed out that he was not unfamiliar with the district. His elder brother had been an assistant minister in an Ayrshire parish before his health had forced him to emigrate to South Africa and, even earlier, in 1822, his grandfather was assistant in West Kilbride. In starting out on his ministry in Largs, Gavin Pagan pledged himself to three main objects: that he and the people of the Parish would get to know each other and become friends; that within the recognised forms of worship he would strive to make his services dignified and meaningful; and that he would maintain and develop the congregational organisations that would give life to the Church. In the short time he was in Largs he was to achieve them all.

He brought to his work the vigour and enthusiasm of youth and a talent for administration. Almost immediately after his arrival he organised a group of ladies to keep members of the congregation in touch with Church affairs as they delivered magazines. The personnel constantly changed and the numbers steadily increased but the aims and methods that Gavin Pagan set out for his Lady Visitors remained in force for more than forty years. In 1903 the traditional "separate tables" gave place to simultaneous serving at the quarterly Communion Services and in the same year the Sunday School was re-organised with John Brown MA as Superintendent and Miss Smith as Primary Leader. This was followed in 1905 by the inauguration of a children's Flower Service. In 1903, a Work Party was formed. It brought the fellowship of regular sewing meetings to the women of the congregation and their Sales of Work raised considerable sums for the work of the Church at home and abroad.

In 1904 the memorial plaque to John Keith was dedicated, and a Church Improvement Scheme re-designed the choir area on a more convenient plan. Outside of the Church, the rough track from Warren Park to the Bowen Craig had been a favourite walk and in the winter of 1905/6 the Largs Visitors' Club provided employment for a number of out of work men by having it transformed into a pleasant pathway.

But the world beyond Largs had its attractions for Gavin Pagan. Simla was an important centre of the British Army and of the civil administration of India, and Europeans flocked to it when the hot season made the plains intolerable to them.

The Scottish Church set considerable store by its representation there and it was something of an honour for any minister to be temporarily assigned to it. In 1907 the Colonial Committee of the Church invited Gavin Pagan to serve at Simla for one year and, after obtaining leave of absence from the Presbytery and his own Church, he left for India in September 1907. He returned in December of the following year, promising that he would do his best not to talk incessantly about his Indian experiences.

However, his congregation hardly had time to become bored with his reminiscences. Within a few months he had accepted a call from St George's Edinburgh, and left Largs in October 1909.

In 1914 Gavin Pagan enlisted, not as a chaplain but to serve in the combatant ranks as a private. He was soon commissioned and on 12th August 1915 he married Mabel, daughter of Gordon Douglas, manager of the Life Association of Scotland. Captain Gavin Lang

Pagan of the 15th Royal Scots was killed in action at Arras on 28th April, 1917. In 1924 a commemorative window, the work of Douglas Strachan, was installed in Largs Church. It portrays the passage in *The Pilgrim's Progress* where Mr Valiant-for-truth takes leave of his friends and crosses the river; and in the scroll at the top of the left light, his farewell words are recalled:

> "My Sword I give to him that shall succeed me in my Pilgrimage, and my Courage and Skill to him that can get it. My Marks and Scars I carry with me, to be a Witness for me, that I have fought his Battles, who now will be my Rewarder".

In 1927 his widow married the Rev. Cecil Thornton of St Margaret's Church, Edinburgh. Gavin Pagan's sword was presented to St George's as a memorial of him.

Gavin Pagan's association with Largs did not end with his death. His parents had retired to Largs in 1908. His father died at the Manse on 21st January 1909, but his mother and his sister Anna lived for many years at Southfield and took the greatest interest in the Church. Mrs Pagan died on 15th August 1933.

Anna Marshall Pagan was secretary of the Vacancy Committee appointed in 1928 and a founder member of the branch of the Woman's Guild. She died on 1st December 1971, at the age of 93.

ROBERT OSWALD

The minister appointed in 1910 could hardly have provided a greater contrast to his predecessor. An older man than Gavin Pagan, he was married with a young family and his experience in building up a new church and in social work seemed to have little relevance to the duties he would be called on to carry out in Largs.

Robert Oswald, the son of John Oswald, Fee Stamp Distributor, and Christina Smart was born at Edinburgh on 6th September, 1864. He was educated at George Watson's College and Edinburgh University, where he graduated Master of Arts in 1886 and Bachelor of Divinity in 1892. Licensed by the Presbytery of Edinburgh on 21st May 1888, he served as assistant in Ardwell Mission Church and in St Andrew's, Edinburgh before being ordained on 28th July 1896, at St Stephen's Chapel, Perth. This was a new charge which had then only 67 members but as a result of his efforts, membership increased; funds were raised; Church buildings improved; and congregational organisations formed; so that it was, within a few years, raised to the full status of a *quoad sacra* parish. In addition, Robert Oswald served as a chaplain to Perth Prison. On 30th June 1903, he married Isabel Fleming, daughter of Robert Pinkerton of Perth and they had a family of three: Helen Dorothy born 2nd October 1904, who married Dr D N A Harrison of London on 25th June, 1932; John, born 2nd April 1908; and Isabel Christian born on 5th September, 1910.

Robert Oswald was translated to Largs on 9th March, 1910. It was said of him that he performed his pastoral duties with "zeal and unselfishness". Certainly, he had considerable organising ability and a keen interest in social work. He was passionately devoted to the cause of temperance and travelled widely to speak on this subject all over the country. At Perth in 1905 he had published a *Memorandum on Reformatory Work among Inebriates*. In 1913 he inaugurated a branch of the Band of Hope in Largs Parish Church and he campaigned vigorously, though in vain, to persuade his Session to accept unfermented wine for Communions. He took great interest in local affairs, serving as Chairman of the Lifeboat Association and being closely connected with the Freemasons.

Within the Church he encouraged and extended the work of the congregational organisations. The Guild, inaugurated by Gavin Pagan in 1903, was revitalised to provide mid-week fellowship for members; and in 1912, William Murray formed a company of Boy Scouts, though it was not until 1918 that the Girl Guides company followed. It was Robert Oswald who initiated the elders' annual visits conveying the good wishes of the Kirk Session to the various organisations and reporting back on the work being done.

Quite early in Robert Oswald's ministry, the Church became concerned about the piece of waste ground in front of Nelson House at the corner of Nelson Street and the Gallowgate. Obviously any development of the site would have gravely detracted from the appearance of the Church. It required long and costly negotiations lasting for almost fifteen years before title to the ground was acquired as a result of the liberality of the congregation and especially of T Cuthbert Stewart of Blackhouse.

But the events that were to have the greatest impact on the parish during Robert Oswald's ministry took place furth of Largs. The outbreak of war inevitably had a profound effect on local life. Robert Oswald volunteered for duty as an army chaplain and in December 1914 handed his pulpit over to the Rev. James Scott BD, while he undertook a three months' tour of duty with the Highland Brigade at Bedford Barracks. He returned to Largs in March 1915, but left again in August to act as chaplain to the Lowland Mounted Brigade. Stationed at Cupar with the rank of Lieutenant-Colonel, he ministered to some 1,500 men in three camps scattered over nine miles, conducting often as many as four or five services each Sunday. After three months he intimated that he would be prepared to undertake a further spell of duty. Although he was informed by the War Office that chaplains were on the same footing as other officers whose service could be enforced, he always prided himself that he served as a volunteer and not by compulsion. His work as an army chaplain seems to have been appreciated, for some units requested that he should accompany them abroad though this proved impossible since he was already over the age for service overseas. During his leaves he returned to Largs to occupy his own pulpit where the Rev. R T Sievewright MA deputised for him in his absence. Robert Oswald's military career ended because of ill-health in July 1916. He returned to Largs where he devoted himself to the onerous pastoral care of a congregation in war-time, and to raising funds for the relief of Belgian refugees, a cause in which he became very active.

The Burgh's official Thanksgiving Service was held in the Parish Church and plans were made for the erection of a suitable War Memorial. In 1919, A H Eckford of St Andrews, presented a stained glass window for the west end of the south aisle in memory of his parents Alexander Haldane Eckford, for many years an elder in the Church and Sunday School Superintendent, and Elizabeth Kerr. It represented Christ walking on the water and was designed and executed by Douglas Strachan, the foremost stained glass artist of the time in Scotland.

As a result, it was decided that Douglas Strachan should be commissioned to provide windows to commemorate the men of the parish who had been killed in the war, and also Gavin Lang Pagan. The latter, at the east end of the south aisle, was designed in scale and arrangement of the subject to complement the Eckford window. The seven light window of the south transept formed the principal war memorial and had as its subject David as a war leader; the central feature being his offering the water from the Bethlehem well to God, since it had been secured at the cost of too many brave men's blood to be used for common purposes. On a pillar near the window was placed a bronze plaque designed by Sir Robert Lorimer and executed by Charles Henshaw of Edinburgh on which are inscribed the names of the ninety-one men of the Parish of Largs who fell in the First World War. The memorials were unveiled and dedicated at a service on the afternoon of Sunday, 7th September 1924. Robert Oswald officiated, assisted by the Rev. James W Gardner of Clark Memorial Church and the Rev. T Birnie Noble of St John's Church and many of the notables of the Burgh took part in the order of service.

A companion piece for the seven light window of the north transept was designed by Douglas Strachan to illustrate the 23rd Psalm; showing on the left the flock being led out to the green pastures and, after passing through the valley of the shadow, finally arriving safely in the fold at nightfall. It was the gift in 1925 of Lady Hope of Dunbar and Mrs Hope of Haddington in memory of their parents Robert Kerr Holms-Kerr and Margaret Ralston.

The range of Douglas Strachan windows in the south aisle was completed in 1938 by his representation of the healing pool at Bethesda which was presented by Miss Katherine MacGregor of Glen Eldon, in memory of her parents Dr George MacGregor and Jane Hamilton. As a result, the Church has a remarkable, perhaps even unique, collection of the artistic work of Douglas Strachan; who is chiefly remembered for his windows in the national Shrine of Remembrance at Edinburgh Castle.

The war had interrupted a process which was fundamentally to change the Parish of Largs. When the Disruption caused controversy and antagonism, there were many on both sides of the division who deplored it and were anxious to work towards its resolution. As early as 1870 the General Assembly of the Established Church placed on record its

> "desire to take all possible steps consistently with the principles on which the Church is founded to promote the reunion of Churches having a common origin."

The only result of this resolution was that it brought the subject into the open as a matter for discussion at least. In 1900, the United Presbyterian and Free Churches united to form the United Free Church and though this had no direct consequence for the Established Church, it could not fail to have an effect on public opinion in Largs. For one thing Robert Rainy, the Principal of New College, Edinburgh, who was one of the chief promoters of the union was by no means a remote, unfamiliar figure. He was the son of Harry Rainy, Professor of Forensic Medicine at Glasgow University, and there were more than a few people who recalled his boyish escapades when he spent holidays with his aunt Margaret Parker in Fairlie. And, once the union was achieved, the sight of the two United Free Churches side by side in Bath Street and working together within the frame-work of a nation-wide organisation, yet each retaining its individual identity and traditions, brought a realisation that unity need not necessarily mean uniformity.

By the 20th century, the issues that had caused the fragmentisation of the Scottish Church no longer existed. The two main streams of Presbyterianism were separated only by the principle of Establishment. It was, however, a formidable obstacle. The "Church by law established" had as its mission the provision of religious ordinances, not for its own members and adherents only, but for all throughout the country who had no other church affiliation; and many people sincerely believed that this immense objective was possible only with the support of the State. On the other hand, the United Free Church could see no scriptural warrant for subordinating the Church to the State and not unnaturally felt that the Established Church with its legally bound heritors and what remained of the old teinds had an unfair financial advantage. Yet it was clear that each Church could make an important contribution towards a potential union. The Established Church had demonstrated its vitality by its recovery from the schism of 1843; the Free Churches had built themselves up from nothing by quite remarkable displays of devotion and liberality. Negotiations between the two Churches began tentatively but by 1909 had reached the stage of "unrestricted conference".

The outbreak of war occasioned some delay but the Articles Declaratory of the Constitution of the Church of Scotland were completed and presented to Parliament in 1921. Both Houses approved the document thus giving the Church national recognition but accepting that freedom to conduct its own affairs was not a matter for civil legislation but was inherent in the constitution of the Church itself. There was a long and complicated legal process to work out a financial settlement. The title to Church property had to be conveyed to the trustees of the Church of Scotland; endowments resulting from the historic teinds had to be promulgated and the heritors had to be relieved at the same time of both their liabilities and privileges. This was finally achieved in the Church of Scotland Properties and Endowments Act of 1925. The way towards reunion was cleared though there remained the immense administrative task of organising the two Churches into a homogeneous whole.

Arrangements for the union were probably less traumatic in Largs than they were in many other parishes. A certain degree of congregational rivalry did certainly exist, but the Presbyterian denominations had an enviable record of helping each other out in emergencies and their ministers on the whole had regarded each other with toleration that bordered on friendship. And, even more important, the Established Church congregation had to some extent anticipated the union by voluntarily surrendering the advantages of establishment when they built and maintained their new Church by their own efforts.

While the local plans for the union were being made, Robert Oswald was granted six months' leave of absence following a heart attack in October 1927. He died on 8th February 1928 and was buried at Haylie following a funeral service in the Church.

On the following Sunday evening, a joint memorial service was held at which the Kirk Sessions of the three Largs Churches attended. In 1931 the congregation installed a memorial window at the east end of the north aisle. Designed by Gordon M Webster of Glasgow, the son of the artist responsible for the window in the south gallery, its theme was the offering to the New Jerusalem of the many and varied gifts from every nation.[24] Mrs Isabel Oswald died in Glasgow in April 1976, in her 96th year.

DAVID BROOK BAXTER.

David Brook Baxter, son of Fred Walker Baxter FRCO, organist and choirmaster, and Laura Brook, was born at Slaithwaite near Huddersfield on 12th June 1898. Educated at Dalry Higher Grade School; Speirs School, Beith; and Glasgow University, he served in the forces in France and from 1917 was a prisoner of war in Germany, where he acted as chaplain to the Protestant prisoners at Munster. He graduated Master of Arts at Glasgow in 1920 and Bachelor of Divinity in 1923. He was ordained at Dunlop in 1923, where he was minister for five years before being translated to Largs. On 27th April 1926, he married Margaret Maitland, daughter of John Barclay, Dalry, and Jessie Cowan McDougall, and had a family of three: Winifred Margaret, who married William Brown Rabey on 25th April 1952; John Barclay Walker[25] and Fred Walker, who married Jean Archibald on 19th June, 1959.

Inducted to Largs Parish Church on 2nd October 1928, David Baxter's arrival coincided with the final arrangements for the union of the Churches. However, in the first year of his ministry an event of some interest in the history of the Parish Church took place. Under the leadership of Mrs Baxter, Miss Anna Marshall Pagan and Miss May S. Donald the long-established Ladies' Work Party was affiliated as a branch of the Woman's Guild of the Church of Scotland. In May 1929 the General Assemblies of the Established Church and the United Free Church met separately for the last time. Both approved the plan for union and on Wednesday 2nd October 1929, the two assemblies became one in a Church of Scotland which, after almost two centuries of schism, united the vast majority of Scottish Presbyterians in a national Church that they believed was free of State interference.

In Largs the congregations of the Parish Church and of the two United Free Churches had accepted the proposed Union. Under it the Parish of Largs was divided into three parts, of which the former Parish Church – to be known subsequently as simply St Columba's Church of Scotland, Largs – retained the northern area, while the southern divisions were assigned to Clark Memorial Church and St John's. On Sunday 29th September, special services were held in the Parish Church to commemorate two events: the first anniversary of David Baxter's ministry in Largs and the closing diets of worship in the old Parish Church. It was, as David Baxter said, a day for looking back to take farewell of the past but at the same time for looking forward, for "the Church must grow, adapt itself and progress otherwise it could have no future".

As at each stage in the reunification of the Church of Scotland there had been a minority not prepared to accept the compromise that change required, so on Sunday 6th October about 70 people – drawn chiefly from the austere secession tradition of Clark Memorial Church, though there were also about half a dozen from St John's – met for worship in Largs Masonic Hall and on the following Tuesday they formally constituted themselves a congregation of the United Free Church of Scotland (Continuing). But on that same Sunday, 6th October 1929, the Rev. David Baxter, the Rev. James Gardner of Clark Memorial Church and Rev. T Birnie Noble of St John's preached from each other's pulpits as a demonstration of their new found unity. On Tuesday 15th October, the new United Presbytery of Ardrossan held its first meeting. Its bounds were from

Largs to Kilwinning, including Beith, Dalry, Glengarnock, Kilbirnie, Millport and Arran – 47 parishes in all.

The story of the Parish of Largs stretched back into the mists of history. After 1929 its future lay with the seven churches – two in Skelmorlie, two in Fairlie and three in Largs – that it had over the years become. The Parish of Largs had ceased to exist as a separate entity, but it can be said of it, as of the burning bush and the Church of Scotland itself,

NEC TAMEN CONSUMEBATUR.

– – – o O o – – –

NOTES

1. No representation or description of the old Church of Largs has survived. The painting in the "Summer" panel on the ceiling of the Skelmorlie Aisle is frequently taken to be of the church, though other features in the paintings are imaginary.
2. The so-called Gallow Hill was identified in 1980 by C J Tabraham, Inspector of Ancient Monuments Department of the Scottish Development Department, as the ruin of a motte and bailey castle. In correspondence with Largs & District Historical Society, Professor G. Barrow pointed out that, since no charters exist for this castle,it was probably retained personally by the de Morville family, superiors of Cunninghame and Largs. Its site close to the old graveyard and the description by John Sheddon-Dobie in his *Church of Largs* p.55 of the church demolished in 1812 as a building "of great strength, the portion remaining being then about four feet in thickness, and of the most compact solidity" may suggest that a church existed in Largs prior to the Norman infiltration, but there is no real evidence for this.
3. There is documentary evidence for the chapels of St Inan at Southannan and St Colm on the Greater Cumbrae. There is a strong local tradition that a chapel dedicated to St Margaret existed on an unknown site at Haylie. If this were so, the Parish of Largs may well be unique in having ancient dedications both to Columba, the founder of the Celtic Church in Scotland, and to Margaret, largely due to whose influence the Celtic Church was superseded in Scotland by the Roman Church. The explanation probably lies in a medieval legend that Margaret, who died in 1093, brought her husband Malcolm and their three sons, four former Kings of Scots, to fight alongside the local levies at the Battle of Largs in 1263. See MacKinley, *Ancient Church*

Dedications in Scotland Non-scriptural, 1914. There is a version of the legend in *Liber Pluscardensis,* as follows:

> "It came to pass at that time that a certain knight, John de Wemyss, Fife, dreamed he went into the church of the blessed Queen Margaret of Scotland at Dunfermline, and saw a queen coming clad in gorgeous aparel of gold, wearing a crown on her head and with her a most comely king, likewise robed in kingly raiment, arrayed in bright armour, wearing a most costly crown on his helmet; and three other kings, equally clad in royal robes and most gorgeously armed, accompanied the foregoing king and queen...So when the said knight beheld them he marvelled, and kneeling down with becoming reverence, said 'O glorious lady I beseech thee deign to show me who thou art and those who accompany thee and whither you are bound'. She said to him with cheerful countenance 'I' said she 'am Margaret Queen of Scotland; he who I lead by the hand is my illustrious husband King Malcolm; the others who follow are my sons whilom kings of this realm; and we are hastening with them to a place called Largs, to defend our country against the snares of the enemy; and God granting us grace we shall gain victory over that tyrant king who is striving wrongfully to invade our realm and subdue it unto him; for as thou knowest I have had this realm entrusted to me and my heirs forever by God'. Then said the knight to her, 'O my glorious lady give me a token whereby I may know this and others may believe me'. ' Go' said she 'to my church of burial and thou shall straightway recover from your sickness'. So the knight who had long been laid up and suffering from some incurable feverish sickness at once woke out of his sleep and made the necessary preparations and failed not to accomplish a pilgrimage on foot to Dunfermline though he could scarcely stir in bed the day before. But when he came to Dunfermline... he was brought to Margaret's bier, touched her relics and prayed; and straightway from that hour he was cured of all his sickness and his fever left him... Shortly afterwards, the king's envoys came thither and brought word of the splendid victory of the battle of Largs."

4. To Mr Baxter's derivation of the placename Kelso may be added the nearby Dochra, which was believed to mean "the priest's house". Local placenames with ecclesiastical connotations can be added to the list, including Annat at Skelmorlie, Chapel Farm at Fairlie and also "the Cannon Lands at Largs" which appear in documents. In the present state of knowledge it is impossible to assess the significance or date of these names. The "Chanty Dyke" in Largs is held by the more genteel to be a corruption of Chantry Dyke, but since the place became a popular rubbish dump the derivation of the name may well be more mundane.

5. The source of the date 1536 has not been traced. The datestone from the original building, now incorporated into the present flats on the site, carries the date 1606, and drawings show the Old Manse to have been a typical small town house of the early 17th century, though undoubtedly there would have been an earlier priest's house either on this site or elsewhere.
6. *Calendar of Papal Registers: Papal Letters I 1198-1304 Ed. Bliss.* I am indebted to M Dilworth, Keeper of the Scottish Catholic Archives for tracing this reference. At one of the lectures he gave in July 1942, Mr Baxter said,
> "Until recently it was believed that the first authentic reference to the Church in Largs was that contained in a Papal Bull of the year 1265....but I have made it my business for some time past carefully to scrutinise numerous old Latin documents...and at this Jubilee Service tonight I desire to make the first intimation of a discovery of some importance: for after patient research I had my reward quite recently – no very great reward it is true, yet a find which made the labour in a sense worthwhile. In short, I came upon a reference in...a Papal Letter written in October 1253 that confirmed to Master William de Kilkenni, Archdeacon of Coventry...the Church of Largis in the Diocese of Glasgow".

7. *Registrum Monasterii de Passelet* pp.227-235; 369- 371.
8. *Calendar of Documents relating to Scotland. Ed. Bain* III,123
9. Several contemporary sources refer to the quarrel between Sempill and the minister of Largs but none gives a reason. It may have had some connection with the guardianship of the Sempill heir.
10. At this point there is some confusion in the list of incumbents. Mr Baxter discovered in an index to the Register of Presentations an entry which read that James Wood was presented as Vicar of Largs Church on 1/4/1576, Mr Alex Wood having resigned. He went to considerable trouble, at a time when the records were dispersed from Edinburgh for safety during the Second World War, to establish that this was an indexing error and referred not to Largs but to Largo in Fife.
Fasti Ecclesiae Scoticanae includes Alexander King as minister of Largs in 1584. This name occurs only once in Mr Baxter's papers in a list of incumbents from which it had afterwards been deleted. There is some implication that Mr Baxter regarded

King – and perhaps also William Fullarton – as temporary placings prior to the appointment of William Cook.
11. *Register of the Great Seal of Scotland, 1580-93,* No.2070.
12. For the Armada wreck see "A Portincross Cannon", by George R. Hewitt in *Ayrshire Archaeological and Natural History Collections Vol. 7* pp 53-57.
13. For information regarding the Spanish Blanks see "The Spanish Blanks and the Catholic Earls" in *Collected Essays and Reviews of Thomas Graves Law.* Ed. Hume Brown. pp 244-276.
14. For the early burghs see "The Burghs of Ayrshire" by George S.Pryde in *Ayrshire Archaeological and Natural History Collections, Vol.4,* p33.
15. This incident is recounted in the *Largs and Millport Weekly News* of 23rd May 1885, and was probably oral tradition by that date.
16. Quotations from Presbytery minutes are from *The Church of Largs* by John Shedden-Dobie.
17. There is some discrepancy in dates. Neil Munro describes Alexander Gordon in 1644 as "a slim elder man" but as portrayed in the novel Gordon displays the combination of severity and humanity which must have characterised many Scottish ministers of the period.
18. Originals of Cumin's call and other 18th century documents quoted are now lost. Fortunately, they were recorded in an unsigned series of articles under the title "The Auld Kirk at Largs" which appeared in the *Largs and Millport Weekly News* from 14th February to 23rd May, 1885. They purported to be derived from "Papers Discovered by David Glen" the Session Clerk, presumably among the Church records entrusted to his care.
19. Dates of birth are as given in *Fasti Ecclesiae Scotticanae* but are obviously in error at least with regard to Thomas. The history of Gilbert Lang's family is not easy to discover for there were at least two other families in Largs named Lang and their exact relationships are very difficult to disentangle.

20. In the mid-19th century, Robert Reid under the pseudonym "Senex", contributed a series of articles about his boyhood in Glasgow to the *Glasgow Herald*. These were collected in *Glasgow Past and Present* published by David Robertson & Co 1884, where in Vol. I pp 425-433, "My third trip to the coast" describes the family holiday in Largs.
21. The small estate of Underbank became afterwards the site of the Hollywood Hotel and now of the Hollywood and Underbank flats.
22. The manse completed in 1886 was demolished in 1957.
23. It is not clear whether the bride was the lady who officiated at the harmonium in the Church Hall because, as is well known, the population of 19th century Largs consisted of the rich and the poor and the Houstons!
24. The windows of the north aisle are all by Gordon Webster. Descriptions of them, and of other gifts to the Church after 1929, can be found in the excellent *Brief Guide for the Use of Visitors* issued by the Church. It has been invaluable in preparing this work.
25. John Barclay Walker Baxter died in Harare, Zimbabwe on 28th July 1987.

---oOo---

PRECENTORS AND ORGANISTS

JAMES THOMSON was precentor in 1810 and served until 1812 at a salary of £4 per annum.

WILLIAM HENDERSON served from 1814 until 1826, his salary being 4 guineas, subsequently raised to 5, per annum.

JOHN BARKLAY was appointed in 1826 at a salary of £10 per annum. The records show that in the years 1830 and 1831 several people acted as Deputy Precentors including Wm Broadfoot, Wm Tyre, Archd Hill, Robert McNeil (grandfather of Robert Beck, a later precentor), John McNeil, and Wm Malcolm. Barklay's appointment ended in 1831.

WILLIAM SHEDDEN was appointed in September, 1831. He was dismissed on 23rd March 1845, and died of cholera in 1849.

JOHN BAYNE who was appointed on 23rd March 1845, came, like the Rev. John Kinross, from St Thomas's, Leith. His salary was £15 per annum, but some trouble arose over his failure to pay two of the "singers in his band". The Kirk Session terminated his appointment on 28th May 1848, and John Hill acted as Interim Precentor. On 28th March 1849, it was decided to advertise for a successor. Applicants were required to produce certificates and Mr Lithgow of Glasgow would be adjudicator.

JOHN ANDERSON from Hamilton was appointed on 4th September, 1849. In 1851 he had a barber's shop in Main Street, Largs. The Church records show that on 24th November 1852, a payment of £3 was made to Robert Kerr "for precenting and otherwise aiding at Gaelic meetings for the last 6 months". The earliest reference to a choir is made in June 1860, when Music Books for its use were purchased from the Proclamation Dues. The Kirk Session terminated Anderson's appointment in August 1862.

Joseph Wood and John Hill were to be paid 5 shillings per Sunday as Interim Singers and a short leet of three applicants for the vacancy was chosen.

HUGH SHEDDEN, a weaver to trade and a bowler of some repute, was appointed in October, 1862. His salary was £20 per year and his duties included making Proclamations and Intimations. In December 1862, the Kirk Session agreed to furnish him with suitable "Names of Tunes". In November 1866, the Kirk Session refused an application for a grant towards a Choir Social but relented sufficiently in the following month to allow the purchase of Music Books to the value of 18 shillings. Shedden resigned in February 1869 and the Kirk Session selected from 24 applicants a short leet of 10 to sing on Sundays. The congregation reduced these to three, who were sent for examination by Mr Lithgow of Glasgow.

WILLIAM A TOWNLEY, a painter to trade and a clarinetist, was appointed from these applicants in June 1869, at a salary of £20 per annum. In April 1873, there were, for the second time, complaints of his neglect of lesser teaching duties in schools and three elders were appointed to co-operate with him in improving the Psalmody. Townley was dismissed in July 1874, and a successor, who, it was stipulated, must be resident in Largs, was sought by advertisement at a salary of £40. In August 1874, it was decided that 7 of the 19 applicants should be heard.

KENNETH McPHERSON, formerly Precentor of Renfrew Free Church, was chosen from the applicants on 30th October, 1874. He kept a butcher's shop where the Royal Oak now stands. In 1875, and again in 1879, the choir seating was re-arranged and a singing class was conducted in 1877. McPherson resigned in January 1883, and the Kirk Session decided to interview Robert Beck for the vacancy.

ROBERT BECK was appointed Precentor in February 1883, at the salary of £20 per annum. Throughout his office he continued to read the Proclamations and Intimations. In March 1885, the Kirk Session decided to introduce the *Scottish Hymnal* and to change the posture for praise and prayer. At the same time it was agreed to make a gift of £10 to Robert Beck on the occasion of his marriage.

In November 1889, it was decided to introduce instrumental music when the new church was erected and this was intimated to the congregation and Presbytery, though the office of Precentor was to be retained until that date. A letter of resignation was received from Beck on 29th June 1892, and the Kirk Session minuted their appreciation of his services and voted a gift of £10 to him.

ROBERT FOX FREW Mus. Doc. The earliest appointment of an organist was of Samuel H. Broughton of St James's, Blackburn, but as he subsequently withdrew his application, the Kirk Session appointed Robert F Frew on 2nd December 1892, at a salary of £80 per annum. He added considerably to the musical culture of the town and in 1893 introduced the *Scottish Anthem Book* into the services of the Church. He resigned in September 1894, and later gained some distinction as organist of Govan Parish Church. He died in Edinburgh in March 1941 aged 78.

GEORGE F. HOWELLS ARCO. Applications for the vacant post of organist exceeded 160 and eventually from them, George Howells of Blairgowrie was appointed on 10th September,1894. He introduced occasional recitals at the end of the evening services and in 1897 Handel's "Messiah" was produced in the Church. In 1898 Largs Choral Society, under his direction, gave a concert in the Stewart Memorial Hall. In 1899 he resigned to take up a similar appointment in Queen Ann Street, Dunfermline. He died in 1943.

ARTHUR D. CURRIE FRCO. On 7th May 1899, Arthur Currie succeeded as organist at the reduced salary of £60 per annum, although this was within a few years restored to the former sum of £80. A growing sense of the importance of the Church Praise was reflected by the introduction of the new *Church Hymnary*, which was to serve for over thirty years, and by the inception of a Choir Social grant; both in 1899. Arthur Currie continued the series of organ recitals inaugurated by his predecessor and served for almost thirteen years under three different ministers until his resignation in March, 1913.

WILLIAM N. MACQUARRIE ARCO. Some difficulty was experienced in filling the vacant post. Mr J W Armitage of Alloa was appointed but refused the post on the grounds that the salary of

£60 per annum – even if increased to £70 – was inadequate. Mr Gerald A Birch accepted £60, but after only a few months had to resign due to ill health. Eventually William N MacQuarrie was appointed at a salary of £70, though it was in the following year increased to £80. In December 1915 he was granted three months' leave of absence to play at Palm Beach, Florida, and in the following year he left temporarily, to take up war service. In 1917 Robert Beck and William Wright received presentations in recognition of their jubilees as choir members. They returned the sums of money they had received to form the Beck-Wright Fund for the provision of music for the choir. On his return from military service, William MacQuarrie's salary was raised to £120 per annum and in February 1923 a new set of Choir Books was presented by William Wright. William MacQuarrie left in 1925 to become organist of Strathbungo Parish Church Glasgow. He was subsequently music master at Marr College, Troon.

JOSEPH W OAKLEY. Following William MacQuarrie's resignation, there were two brief appointments. H C Jeffrey ARCO. began duty in the latter part of 1925 but gave up before the end of the year to be followed by George F Walker of Campbeltown who left in less than three months for family and business reasons. Joseph Oakley was appointed in April 1926, and took up office in the late summer. He successfully conducted a Glee Club in addition to the Church Choir and maintained a Junior Choir throughout his appointment. In 1933, the *Revised Church Hymnary* of 1927 was introduced. While in Largs, Joseph Oakley took the diplomas of ARCM and LRAM. He resigned in 1950 and was later organist at Merrylee in Glasgow, and at Mearnskirk.

---oOo---

APPENDIX

Inevitably, celebration of the Golden Jubilee of the dedication of St Columba's Church was restricted by the Second World War. The windows, one of the glories of the building, had been removed for safe keeping; many of the congregation were absent from Largs on war service and not a few of those who had contributed to the progress of the Church over its fifty years of life had commitments which prevented them from returning to take part in the ceremonies. Yet, in spite of these difficulties, the office-bearers and congregation contrived to make July 1942 memorable in the history of the Church.

What was described in the local press as the first of "a noteworthy series of services" was held on Sunday, 5th July. At the morning service the preacher was the Rev. John Heggie of Barry West Church, who had from 1892 to 1895 been the first assistant minister and who paid tribute to Dr John Keith. George F Howells ARCO, of Dunfermline led the praise at the organ. Of the five organists who had served the Church, Robert Frew had died, but each of the other four was invited, on one Sunday in July, to play the magnificent Willis organ during worship and to give a recital at the close of the evening service. Robert Beck, the former Precentor, had a few years earlier retired from the choir but he took his long-accustomed place among the basses for the services of the Jubilee month.

It was typical of David Baxter that he was determined to honour not a mere fifty years-old building, but a much more ancient heritage. At the evening service he said:

> "In commemorating this the third Parish Church in Largs let us not forget its original precursors and the faithful men and women who worshipped and served the same Lord here in this place whom we now serve"

and he gave an address summarising the history of the Church in Largs from the earliest times to the Reformation.

The services on the 12th July followed the same pattern. The Rev. James H Gillespie of Dundonald, who had been assistant minister from 1895 to 1900, preached at the morning service. It had been hoped that Arthur D Currie FRCO would play the organ, but he was prevented from doing so by an accident and the church organist Joseph W Oakley had to deputise for him at short notice. At the evening service in an address which he entitled "Fifty Year in Retrospect", David Baxter gave an account of the progress and development of the Church since 1892. He took some pride in the fact that during his ministry the congregation had doubled in size, but he said little of his own activities for he had no wish to impinge on "a Jubilee which is not mine but yours."

He concluded his remarks with the words:

> "And so my story ends: or rather does not end, for the work yet goes on and with God's blessing shall still go on and prosper. We have much to be proud of: yet let none of us be too proud but rather humbly devoted, far removed from self- seeking and from loving the praise of men more than the praise of God. For of a truth John Keith planted and planted right well. Gavin Lang Pagan and Robert Oswald and you and I and the great unsung multitude whose names are in the book of life watered. But it is God alone who giveth the increase. 'Not unto us, O Lord, not unto us, but unto Thy name give glory for Thy mercy and Thy truth's sake.'"

The Jubilee Thanksgiving Service took place on the morning of Sunday 19th July. The Right Rev. C W G Taylor officiated. He was Moderator of the General Assembly and had succeeded Gavin Lang Pagan at St George's, Edinburgh. He was assisted by the Rev. David Baxter and the Rev. David McArthur, the assistant minister. J W Oakley led the praise at the organ and among the many guests were Andrew Balfour, the architect of the Church, and Mrs Oswald.

One member of the Kirk Session was unavoidably absent, but Gunner Alistair Brown had sent his good wishes by letter. Special invitations had been sent to those of the congregation, thirty-three in number – among them about eight who had been first communicants during the ministry of John Kinross – who had been members throughout the half century of the lifetime of the Church, and it was a joy to both minister and congregation that so many of them were able to attend the Service.

Apologies for absence were received from James Crawford and Miss Mary Crawford of Raillies and Mrs Thomas Fraser of 79 Nelson Street, but taking their place of honour alongside the Kirk Session were:-John Wilson, Meadow Bank, the Senior Elder; Robert Beck, Thistle Cottage, the last Precentor; Miss Hill, Rowanlea, 33 Wilson Street; Miss Smith, Newton Bank, Douglas Street; Miss Margaret Anderson, Mayfield, May Street; Miss Elizabeth J Anderson, Mayfield, May Street; Miss Wright, Mount Charles, Cathcart Road; Miss Elizabeth B Carswell, 28 Gateside Street; Miss Eliza Hopkirk, Feodora, Lovat Street; Mrs Campbell, Glendale, 9 Sinclair Drive; Mr and Mrs Robert Frazer, Struan, Lovat Street; Mrs D Lang, 28 Frazer Street; Miss Lang, 50 Nelson Street; Mrs Henderson, 6 Nelson Street; Mrs George E Marshall, Gallowhill Place; Miss Jemima Halliday, Moorburn Cottage; Mrs Martindale, 140 Main Street; Mr and Mrs William Crawford, Burnside Cottages; and Mr David Crawford, 43 Gateside Street.

In a brief ceremony in the Session House at the close of the service the Moderator presented an inscribed Bible to David Baxter in recognition of his fourteen years of service to the parish and congregation. At the same time Bibles were presented to John S Wilson, the Senior Elder, Alexander K Edward, the Session Clerk and Robert Cromarty, the Treasurer, as an appreciation of their personal services to the Church but also as a symbol of the great debt owed to all the office-bearers of the past. A Service of Holy Communion was held in the evening.

The Jubilee celebrations came to a close on Sunday, 26th July. The Rev. Ludovic W C Grey of Tillicoultry, assistant minister from 1938 to 1940, officiated and William N Macquarrie led the praise at the organ. The annual Children's Flower Service was usually held in June but it had been postponed so that the children in the Sunday School and youth groups would understand something of the greatness of their heritage by playing a part in the celebration. Each child was presented with an illustrated Jubilee Testament provided from a legacy of Miss Katherine MacGregor of Glen Eldon and tribute was paid to the past work of the Sunday School and its many faithful teachers. In his talk to the children David Baxter reminded them that though they met then to remember the past, by God's grace many of them would live to see the hundredth birthday of the Church and he asked them all to prepare for that, so that the Church after 100 years would be even stronger than it had shown itself to be after fifty.

The centenary of the Church lay far in the future but there was another anniversary much closer in time. It is clear from his papers that David Baxter saw the Covenants as the epic period in the history of the Scottish Church. He delighted to imagine the people of Largs, laird's wife and labourer, trudging up the glen to attend conventicles on the moor though, as a historian, he knew that there was neither evidence nor tradition of any such events.

He admired the Rev. John Wallace though he well knew that his stand was no more than that of most ministers of the time. In his heart David Baxter regretted that Largs had no Covenanting martyr and so he transferred his esteem to a minister who died not for some highly charged emotional cause, but in the routine performance of his duty to his parishioners.

The disease which broke out in Scotland in the mid-17th century is often referred to as bubonic plague or cholera, but in fact it was neither. Modern medical opinion considers it to have been typhus similar to that which spread over continental Europe during the Thirty Years' War – perhaps even the same infection. Most epidemics had their worst effects in the crowded insanitary conditions of the towns but it was noted that this illness was equally lethal in country districts, following the armies of Royalist and Covenanter as they marched and counter-marched across Scotland. How it reached Largs will never be known, but "the plague", and the young minister who became its victim, left an abiding impression on the folk memory of the town.

It was during the Diamond Jubilee celebrations that David Baxter first spoke of what was to become one of his dearest wishes:

> "As to the present conditions of the Prophet's Grave there is much that one could say. It finds mention in the local guide-books as one of the sights commended to our summer visitors. And "a sight" it truly is, but in another

Re-dedication of the Prophet's Grave, 20th May, 1956. Left to right: Alex. Simpson; Rev. D. B. Baxter; J. Macpherson; J. Campbell; D. Brown; T. Speaker; G. Arkison; Provost J. Robertson; Mrs Young; ---.

sense than that of the guide-books. Old photographs show the tombstone resting on four supporting pillars. These have long since disappeared and the flat slab now rests unevenly on an undressed grassy slope. Though but a short distance from the roadway, there is no proper access available and probably most of those who do go in search of the grave are turned back from the fruitless quest. Largs has no standing memorials to its Covenanting forefathers, no martyr graves in the accepted sense. Yet here is a true martyr's grave which is all our own and ought to be the peculiar pride not only of Largs, but especially of the Church in which William Smith ministered; the Church for which he laid down his life in the pestilence, a martyr to his high pastoral calling. I am no prophet nor son of a prophet but if I were, I should like to hazard another prophecy for the coming days of peace. September 1947 will be the tercentenary of William Smith's death, and the vision I cherish against the day is this: a congregation of the Parish Church of Largs raising funds for the restoration of the Prophet's Grave; a committee of its Kirk Session seeking from the proprietor liberty to construct a seemly entrance to a well cared-for memorial; a loyal people supporting their appeal with spiritual imagination and material assistance; and all the funds raised and the work so far advanced that on a lovely autumn afternoon of 1947 the grateful parishioners of Largs shall go on pilgrimage to the Brisbane Glen and, led by the Parish Minister of the day, take part in a great open-air service around that hallowed and beautiful spot commemorating, amid worthy surroundings, William Smith of the Prophet's Grave, the Martyr-Minister of Largs."

The tercentenary came too soon after the end of the war for anything other than a token fulfilment of this dream. It was not until Sunday, 20th May 1956, that the people of Largs headed by the local clergy and the Provost and councillors of the Burgh met; not on the sunny afternoon David Baxter had envisaged, but on a blustery day of heavy rain, to re-dedicate the restored Prophet's Grave. A sum of £372 6s 5d had been raised; enough to construct an access pathway, to tidy the site and to provide a brass plaque engraved with the epitaph from the original stone. There was a short religious service at which psalms were sung to 17th century tunes with Alex Simpson, Session Clerk of St John's Church, acting as precentor. Alexander Hill, described as "one of the senior native elders of the Church of Scotland in Largs", unveiled the plaque by removing the saltire flag which covered it and it was formally dedicated. In his address, David Baxter gave a brief account of the events that had led up to the ceremony and some of those who had helped to bring it about:

"First my own congregation, direct successor to William Smith's, took up the matter and in a short time by private subscription and donations had over £100 in hand for the work. Next, the assistance of Largs Business Club was enlisted with Mr Alex Simpson, its Secretary, assiduously keeping the project before its members. Local interest was widened and many well-wishers readily co-operated, until today we find ourselves with a considerable part of our plans carried through. There are many we should like to thank, but cannot; and some whose special assistance must be acknowledged. Mr John Campbell of Auchengarth, for generously giving the site with land for making the access path; Messrs Mackie, Blacksmiths, for the entrance gate of wrought iron; and Mr James Guthrie for painting it; Mr Alexander Campbell for erecting the gate pillars; the planning committee from St Columba's Church and Largs Business Club; Mr Joseph Campbell, the Parks Superintendent, for his expert advice on the lay-out of the site and for his general supervision of the work of restoration; the Provost, Magistrates and members of Largs Town Council for their interest and encouragement and for their promise to take over the site when completed; and not least, all who have subscribed the funds to advance the project. We trust the community will once again make this a place of pleasant pilgrimage and will help to safeguard it as a hallowed spot."

---oOo---